QUEEN MAB

A PHILOSOPHICAL POEM

BY

PERCY BYSSHE SHELEY

Polilaudanum Press

QUEEN MAB

By Percy Bysshe Shelley

Edited By Kay Hawkins

Toronto, Canada

2019

ACKNOWLEDGEMENTS

Thank you to Robarts Library and the University of Toronto for providing me with the resources I needed to make this book possible, and for all the learning and support I've received there.

INTORDUCTION

What you are about to read has been part of an ongoing passion project of mine, in which I modernize the writings of my favorite authors by republishing their original texts in a more contemporary style. The first in this project is Queen Mab, a wonderful poem originally by Percy Bysshe Shelley. This edition stays as close to the original format as possible, including all the original notes by Percy Shelley as he had intended. My vision for this project was to take the author's work exactly as it was, while answering the question, "What if this were written today?"
Queen Mab was written by one of my personal favorite minds in history. This is my way of honoring him, and spreading his message and his wisdom to the world today.
RIP Shelley

To HARRIET

Whose is the love that gleaming through the
world,
Wards off the poisonous arrow of its scorn?
Whose is the warm and partial praise,
Virtue's most sweet reward?
Beneath whose looks did my reviving soul
Ripen in truth and virtuous daring grow?
Whose eyes have I gazed fondly on,
And loved mankind the more?
HARRIET! on thine:—thou wast my purer
mind;
Thou wast the inspiration of my song;
Thine are these early winding flowers,
Then press unto thy breast this pledge of love,
And know, though time may change, and years
may roll,
Each floweret gathered in my heart
It consecrates to thine.

8

QUEEN MAB

1

How wonderful is Death,
Death and his brother Sleep!
One, pale as yonder waning moon
With lips of lurid blue;
The other, rosy as the morn
When throned on ocean's wave
It blushes o'er the world:
Yet both so passing wonderful!

Hath then the gloomy Power
Whose reign is in the tainted sepulchres
Seized on her sinless soul?
Must then that peerless form
Which love and admiration cannot view
Without a beating heart, those azure veins
Which steal like streams along a field of snow,
That lovely outline, which is fair
As breathing marble, perish?
Must putrefaction's breath
Leave nothing of this heavenly sight
But loathsomeness and ruin?
Spare nothing but a gloomy theme,
On which the lightest heart might moralize?
Or is it only a sweet slumber
Stealing o'er sensation,
Which the breath of roseate morning
Chaseth into darkness?
Will Ianthe wake again,
And give that faithful bosom joy
Whose sleepless spirit waits to catch
Light, life, and rapture from her smile?

Yes! she will wake again,
Although her glowing limbs are motionless,
And silent those sweet lips,
Once breathing eloquence
That might have soothed a tyger's rage,
Or thawed the cold heart of a conqueror.
Her dewy eyes are closed,
And on their lids, whose texture fine
Scarce hides the dark blue orbs beneath,
The baby Sleep is pillowed:
Her golden tresses shade
The bosom's stainless pride,
Curling like tendrils of the parasite
Around a marble column.

Hark! whence that rushing sound?
'Tis like the wondrous strain
That round a lonely ruin swells,
Which, wandering on the echoing shore,
The enthusiast hears at evening:
'Tis softer than the west wind's sigh;
'Tis wilder than the unmeasured notes
Of that strange lyre whose strings
The genii of the breezes sweep:
Those lines of rainbow light
Are like the moonbeams when they fall
Through some cathedral window, but the teints
Are such as may not find
Comparison on earth.

Behold the chariot of the Fairy Queen!
Celestial coursers paw the unyielding air
Their filmy pennons at her word they furl,
And stop obedient to the reins of light:
These the Queen of Spells drew in,

She spread a charm around the spot,
And leaning graceful from the ethereal car,
Long did she gaze, and silently,
Upon the slumbering maid.

Oh! not the visioned poet in his dreams,
When silvery clouds float through the wildered brain,
When every sight of lovely, wild, and grand,
Astonishes, enraptures, elevates,
When fancy, at a glance, combines
The wondrous and the beautiful,—
So bright, so fair, so wild a shape
Hath ever yet beheld,
As that which reined the coursers of the air,
And poured the magic of her gaze
Upon the maiden's sleep.

The broad and yellow moon
Shone dimly through her form--
That form of faultless symmetry;
The pearly and pellucid car
Moved not the moonlight's line:
'Twas not an earthly pageant:
Those who had looked upon the sight,
Passing all human glory,
Saw not the yellow moon,
Saw not the mortal scene,
Heard not the night-wind's rush,
Heard not an earthly sound,
Saw but the fairy pageant,
Heard but the heavenly strains
That filled the lonely dwelling.

The Fairy's frame was slight, yon fibrous cloud,
That catches but the palest tinge of even,
And which the straining eye can hardly seize

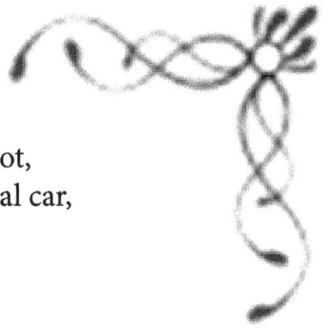

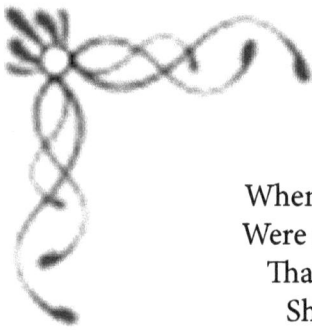

When melting into eastern twilight's shadow,
Were scarce so thin, so slight; but the fair star
That gems the glittering coronet of morn,
Sheds not a light so mild, so powerful,
As that which, bursting from the Fairy's form,
Spread a purpureal halo round the scene,
Yet with an undulating motion,
Swayed to her outline gracefully.
From her celestial car
The Fairy Queen descended,
And thrice she waved her wand
Circled with wreaths of amaranth :
Her thin and misty form
Moved with the moving air,
And the clear silver tones,
As thus she spoke, were such
As are unheard by all but gifted ear.

FAIRY.

Stars! your balmiest influence shed !
Elements! your wrath suspend!
Sleep, Ocean, in the rocky bounds
That circle thy domain!
Let not a breath be seen to stir
Around yon grass-grown ruin's height,
Let even the restless gossamer
Sleep on the moveless air!
Soul of Ianthe ! thou,
Judged alone worthy of the envied boon,
That waits the good and the sincere; that waits
Those who have struggled, and with resolute will
Vanquished earth's pride and meanness,bursts the chains,
The icy chains of custom, and have shone
The day-stars of their age;—Soul of Ianthe !
Awake! arise!

12

Sudden arose
Ianthe's Soul; it stood
All beautiful in naked purity,
The perfect semblance of its bodily frame.
Instinct with inexpressible beauty and grace,
Each stain of earthliness
Had passed away, it reassumed
Its native dignity, and stood
Immortal amid ruin.

Upon the couch the body lay
VV-rapt in the depth of slumber:
Its features were fixed and meaningless,
Yet animal life was there,
And every organ yet performed
Its natural functions: 'twas a sight
Of wonder to behold the body and soul.
The self-same lineaments, the same
Marks of identity were there:
Yet, oh, how different! One aspires to Heaven,
Pants for its sempiternal heritage,
And ever-changing, ever-rising still,
Wantons in endless being.
The other, for a time the unwilling sport
Of circumstance and passion, struggles on;
Fleets through its sad duration rapidly:
Then like an useless and worn-out machine,
Rots, perishes, and passes.

FAIRY.
Spirit! who bast dived so deep ;
Spirit! who hast soared so high;
Thou the fearless, thou the mild,
Accept the boon thy worth hath earned,
Ascend the car with me.

SPIRIT.

Do I dream? Is this new feeling
But a visioned ghost of slumber?
If indeed I am a soul,
A free, a disembodied soul,
Speak again to me.

FAIRY.

I am the Fairy MAB: to me 'tis given
The wonders of the human world to keep:
The secrets of the immeasurable past,
In the unfailing consciences of men,
Those stern, unflattering chroniclers, I find:
The future, from the causes which arise
In each event, I gather: not the sting
Which retributive memory implants
In the hard bosom of the selfish man;
Nor that exta.tic and exulting throb
Which virtue's votary feels when he sums up
The thoughts and actions of a well-spent day,
Are unforeseen, unregistered by me:
And it is yet permitted me, to rend
The veil of mortal frailty, that the spirit
Clothed in its changeless purity, may know
How soonest to accomplish the great end
For which it hath its being, and may taste
That peace, which in the end all life will share.
This is the meed of virtue; happy Soul,
Ascend the car with me!

The chains of earth's immurement
Fell from Ianthe's spirit;
They shrank and break like bandages of straw
Beneath a wakened giant's strength.
She knew her glorious change,

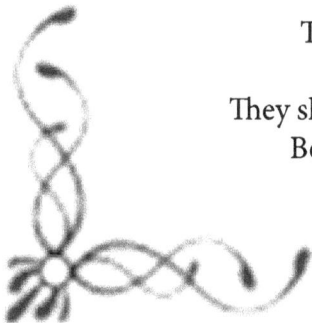

14

And felt in apprehension uncontrolled
New raptures opening round:
Each day-dream of her mortal life,
Each frenzied vision of the slumbers
That closed each well-spent day,
Seemed now to meet reality.

The Fairy and the Soul proceeded;
The silver clouds disparted;
And as the car of magic they ascended,
Again the speechless music swelled,
Again the coursers of the air
Unfurled their azure pennons, and the Queen
Shaking the beamy reins
Bade them pursue their way.

The magic car moved on.
The night was fair, and countless stars
Studded heaven's dark blue vault,—
Just o'er the eastern wave
Peeped the first faint smile of morn :—

The magic car moved on—
From the celestial hoofs
The atmosphere in flaming sparkles flew,
And where the burning wheels
Eddied above the mountain's loftiest peak,
Was traced a line of lightning.
Now it flew far above a rock,
The utmost verge of earth,
The rival of the Andes, Whose dark brow
Lowered o'er the silver sea.

Far, far below the chariot's path,
Calm as a slumbering babe,

Tremendous Ocean lay.
The mirror of its stillness shewed
The pale and waning stars,
The chariot's fiery track,
And the grey light of morn
Tinging those fleecy clouds
That canopied the dawn.
Seemed it, that the chariot's way
Lay through the midst of an immense concave,
Radiant with million constellations, tinged
With shades of infinite colour,
And semicircled with a belt
Flashing incessant meteors.

The magic car moved on.
As they approached their goal
The coursers seemed to gather speed;
The sea no longer was distinguished; earth
Appeared a vast and shadowy sphere;
The sun's unclouded orb
Rolled a-11# the black concave;
Its rays of rapid light
Parted around the chariot's swifter course,
And fell, like ocean's feathery spray
Dashed from the boiling surge
Before a vessel's prow.

The magic car moved on.
Earth's distant orb appeared
The smallest light that twinkles in the heaven;
Whilst round the chariot's way
Innumerable systems rolled,
And countless spheres diffused
An ever-varying glory
It was a sight of wonder: some

Were horned like the crescent moon;
Some shed a mild and silver beam
Like Hesperus o'er the western sea;
Some dash'd athwart with trains of flame,
Like worlds to death and ruin driven;
Some shone like suns, and as the chariot passed,
Eclipsed all other light.

Spirit of Nature! here!
In this interminable wilderness
Of worlds, at whose immensity
Even soaring fancy staggers,
Here is thy fitting temple.
Yet not the lightest leaf

That quivers to the passing breeze
Is less instinct with thee:
Yet not the meanest worm
That lurks in graves and fattens on the dead
Less shares thy eternal breath.
Spirit of Nature! thou!
Imperishable as this scene,
Here is thy fitting temple.

18

II

IF solitude bath ever led thy steps
To the wild ocean's echoing shore,
And thou hast lingered there,
Until the sun's broad orb
Seemed resting on the burnished wave,
Thou must have marked the lines
Of purple gold, that motionless
Hung o'er the sinking sphere:
Thou must have marked the billowy clouds
Edged with intolerable radiancy
Towering like rocks of jet
Crowned with a diamond wreath.
And yet there is a moment,
When the sun's highest point
Peeps like a star o'er ocean's western edge,
When those far clouds of feathery gold,
Shaded with deepest purple, gleam
Like islands on a dark blue sea;
Then has thy fancy soared above the earth,
And furled its wearied wing
Within the Fairy's fane.

Yet not the golden islands
Gleaming in yon flood of light,
Nor the feathery curtains
Stretching o'er the sun's bright couch,
Nor the burnished ocean waves
Paving that gorgeous dome,
So fair, so wonderful a sight
As Mab's ethereal palace could afford.
Yet likest evening's vault, that faery Hall!
As Heaven, low resting on the wave, it spread
Its floors of flashing light,

Its vast and azure dome,
Its fertile golden islands
Floating on a silver sea;
Whilst suns their mingling beamings darted
Through clouds of circumambient darkness,
And pearly battlements around
Looked o'er the immense of Heaven.
The magic car no longer moved.
The Fairy and the Spirit
Entered the Hall of Spells:
Those golden clouds
That rolled in glittering billows
Beneath the azure canopy
With the ethereal footsteps, trembled not:
The light and crimson mists,
Floating to strains of thrilling melody
Through that unearthly dwelling,
Yielded to every movement of the will.
Upon their passive swell the Spirit leaned,
And, for the varied bliss that pressed around,
Used not the glorious privilege
Of virtue and of wisdom.
Spirit! the Fairy said,
And pointed to the gorgeous dome,
This is a wondrous sight
And mocks all human grandeur;
But, were it virtue's only meed, to dwell
In a celestial palace, all resigned
To pleasurable impulses, immured
Within the prison of itself; the will
Of changeless nature would be unfulfilled.
Learn to make others happy. Spirit, come!
This is thine high reward :the past shall rise;
Thou shalt behold the present; I will teach
The secrets of the future.

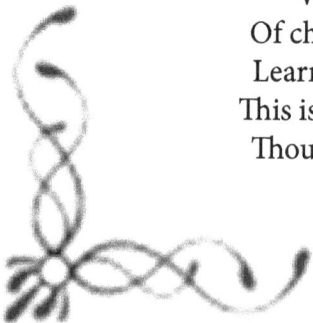

The Fairy and the Spirit
Approached the overhanging battlement.—
Below lay stretched the universe!
There, far as the remotest line
That bounds imagination's flight,
Countless and unending orbs
In mazy motion intermingled,
Yet still fulfilled immutably
Eternal nature's law.
Above, below, around
The circling systems formed
A wilderness of harmony.
Each with undeviating aim,
In eloquent silence, through the depths of space
Pursued its wondrous way.

There was a little light
That twinkled in the misty distance:
None but a spirit's eye
Might ken that rolling orb;
None but a spirit's eye,
And in no other place
But that celestial dwelling, might behold
Each action of this earth's inhabitants.
But matter, space, and time
In those aerial mansions cease to act;
And all-prevailing wisdom, when it reaps
The harvest of its excellence, o'erbounds
Those obstacles, of which an earthly soul
Fears to attempt the conquest.

The Fairy pointed to the earth.
The Spirit's intellectual eye
Its kindred beings recognized.
The thronging thousands, to a passing view,

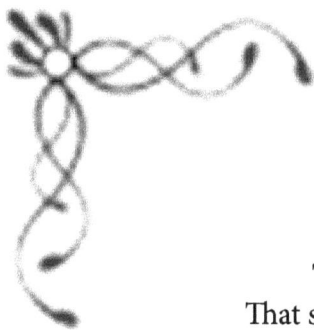

Seemed like an anthill's citizens.
How wonderful! that even
The passions, prejudices, interests,
That sway the meanest being, the weak touch
That moves the finest nerve,
And in one human brain
Causes the faintest thought, becomes a link
In the great chain of nature.

Behold, the Fairy cried.
Palmyra's ruined palaces !—
Behold! where grandeur frowned;
Behold! where pleasure smiled;
What now remains ?—the memory
Of senselessness and shame—
What is immortal there?
Nothing—it stands to tell
A melancholy tale, to give
An awful warning: soon
Oblivion will steal silently
The remnant of its fame.
Monarchs and conquerors there
Proud o'er prostrate millions trod
Theearthquakes of the human race;
Like them, forgotten when the ruin
That marks their shock is past.

Beside the eternal Nile,
The Pyramids have risen.
Nile shall pursue his changeless way:
Those pyramids shall fall;
Yea! not a stone shall stand to tell
The spot whereon they stood;
Their very scite shall be forgotten,
As is their builder's name!

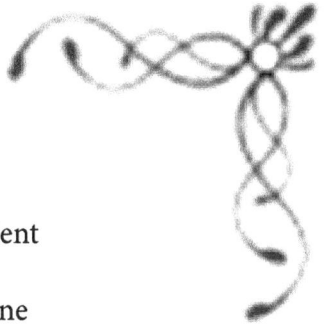

Behold yon sterile Spot;
Where now the wandering Arab's tent
Flaps in the desert blast.
There once old Salem's haughty fane
Reared high to heaven its thousand golden domes,
And in the blushing face of day
Exposed its shameful glory.
Oh! many a widow, many an orphan cursed
The building of that fane ; and many a father,
Worn out with toil And slavery, implored
The poor man's God to sweep it from the earth,
And spare his children the detested task
Of piling stone on stone, and poisoning
The choicest days of life,
To soothe a dotard's vanity.
Their an inhuman and uncultured race
Howled hideous praises to their Demon-God;
They rushed to war, tore from the mother's womb
The unborn child,—old age and infancy
Promiscuous perished; their victorious arms
Left not a soul to breathe. Oh! they were fiends:
But what was he who taught them that the God
Of nature and benevolence had given
A special sanction to the trade of blood?
His name and theirs are fading, and the tales
Of this barbarian nation, which imposture
Recites till terror credits, are pursuing
Itself into forgetfulness.

Where Athens, Rome, and Sparta stood,
There is a moral desert now:
The mean and miserable huts,
The yet more wretched palaces,
Contrasted with those ancient fanes,
Now crumbling to oblivion;

23

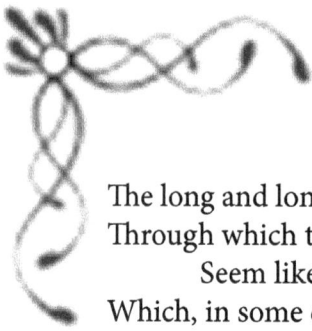

The long and lonely colonnades,
Through which the ghost of Freedom stalks,
      Seem like a well-known tune,
Which, in some dear scene we have loved to hear,
      Remembered now in sadness.
      But, oh! how much more changed,
      How gloomier is the contrast
      Of human nature there!
Where Socrates expired, a tyrant's slave,
A coward and a fool, spreads death around—
      Then, shuddering, meels his own.
Where Cicero and Antoninus lived,
   A cowled and hypocritical monk
      Prays, curses, and deceives.

      Spirit! ten thousand years
      Have scarcely past away,
Since, in the waste where now the savage drinks
His enemy's blood, and aping Europe's sons,
      Wakes the unholy song of war,
      Arose a stately city,
Metropolis of the western continent:
   There, now, the mossy column-stone,
Indented by time's unrelaxing grasp,
      Which once appeared to brave
      All, save its country's ruin;
      There the wide forest scene,
Rude in the uncultivated loveliness
      Of gardens long run wild,
Seems, to the unwilling sojourner, whose steps
   Chance in that desert has delayed,
Thus to have stood since earth was what it is.
   Yet once it was the busiest haunt,
Whither, as to a common centre, flocked
Strangers, and ships, and merchandize

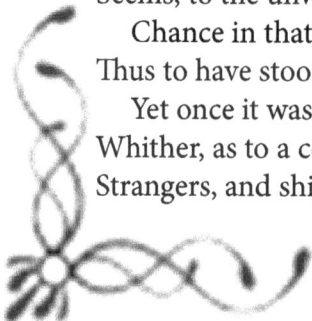

Once peace and freedom blest
The cultivated plain:
But wealth, that curse of man,
Blighted the bud of its prosperity:
Virtue and wisdom, truth and liberty,
Fled, to return not, until man shall know
That they alone can give the bliss
Worthy a soul that claims
Its kindred with eternity.

There's not one atom of yon earth
But once was living man;
Nor the minutest drop of rain,
That hangeth in its thinnest cloud,
But flowed in human veins:
And from the burning plains
Where Lybian monsters yell,
From the most gloomy glens
Of Greenland's sunless clime,
To where the golden fields
Of fertile England spread
Their harvest to the day,
Thou canst not find one spot
Whereon no city stood.

How strange is human pride!
I tell thee that those living things,
To whom the fragile blade of grass,
That springeth in the morn
And perisheth ere noon,

Is an unbounded world;
I tell thee that those viewless beings,
Whose mansion is the smallest particle
Of the impassive atmosphere,
Think, feel, and live like than;
That their affections and antipathies,

Like his, produce the laws
Ruling their moral state;
And the minutest throb
That through their frame diffuses
The slightest, faintest motion,
Is fixed and indispensable
As the majestic laws
That rule yon rolling orbs.

The Fairy paused. The Spirit,
In extacy of admiration, felt
All knowledge of the past revived; the events
Of old and wondrous times,
Which dim tradition interruptedly
Teaches the credulous vulgar, were unfolded
In just perspective to the view;
Yet dim from their infinitude.
The Spirit seemed to stand
High on an isolated pinnacle;
The flood of ages combating below,
The depth of the unbounded universe
Above, and all around
Nature's unchanging harmony.

III

FAIRY! the Spirit said,
  And on the Queen of Spells
  Fixed her ethereal eyes,
I thank thee. Thou hast given
A boon which I will not resign, and taught
A lesson not to be unlearned. I know
The past, and thence I will essay to glean
A warning for the future, so that man
May profit by his errors, and derive
  Experience from his folly:
For, when the power of imparting joy
Is equal to the will, the human soul
  Requires no other heaven.

MA B.

  Turn thee, surpassing Spirit!
  Much yet remains unscanned.
  Thou knowest how great is man,
  Thou knowest his imbecility:
  Yet learn thou what he is;
  Yet learn the lofty destiny
  Which restless time prepares
  For every living soul.
Behold a gorgeous palace, that, amid
Yon populous city, rears its thousand towers
And seems itself a city. Gloomy troops
Of centinels, in stern and silent ranks,
Encompass it around : the dweller there
Cannot be free and happy; hearest thou not
'The curses of the fatherless, the groans
Of those who have no friend? He passes on:
The King, the wearer of a gilded chain

27

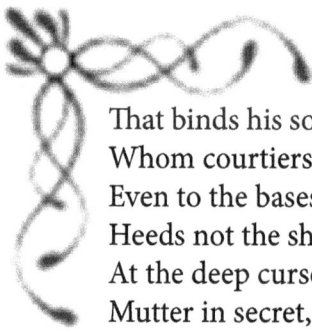

That binds his soul to abjectness, the fool
Whom courtiers nickname monarch, whilst a slave
Even to the basest appetites—that man
Heeds not the shriek of Penury; he smiles
At the deep curses which the destitute
Mutter in secret, and a sullen joy
Pervades his bloodless heart when thousands groan
But for those morsels which his wantonness
Wastes in unjoyous revelry, to save
All that they love from famine: when he hears
The tale of horror, to some ready-made face
Of hypocritical assent he turns,
Smothering the glow of shame, that, spite of him,
Flushes his bloated cheek.

                    Now to the meal
Of silence, grandeur, and excess, he drags
His palled unwilling appetite. If gold,
Gleaming around, and numerous viands culled
From every clime, could force the loathing sense
To overcome satiety,— if wealth
The spring it draws from poisons not,—or vice,
Unfeeling, stubborn vice, converteth not
Its food to deadliest venom; then that king
Is happy; and the peasant who fulfils
His unforced task, when he returns at even,
And by the blazing faggot meets again
Her welcome for whom all his toil is sped,
Tastes not a sweeter meal.

                    Behold him now
Stretched on the gorgeous couch; his fevered brain
Reels dizzily awhile: But, ah! too soon
The slumber of intemperance subsides,
And conscience, that undying serpent, calls
Her venomous brood to their nocturnal task.

KING.

No cessation!
Oh! must this last for ever! Awful death,
I wish, yet fear to clasp thee !—Not one moment
Of dreamless sleep! 0 dear and blessed peace!
Why dost thou shroud thy vestal purity
In penury and dungeons? wherefore lurkest
With danger, death, and solitude; yet shunn'st
The palace I have built thee? Sacred peace!
Oh visit me but once, but pitying shed
One drop of balm upon my withered soul.

Vain man! that palace is the virtuous heart,
And peace defileth not her snowy robes
In such a shed as thine. Hark! yet he mutters;
His slumbers are but varied agonies,
They prey like scorpions on the springs of life.
There neecleth not the hell that bigots frame
To punish those who err: earth in itself
Contains at once the evil and the cure;
And all-sufficing nature can chastise
Those who transgress her law,—she only knows
How justly to proportion to the fault
The punishment it merits.

Is it strange
That this poor wretch should pride him in his woe?
Take pleasure in his abjectness, and hug
The scorpion that consumes him? Is it strange
That, placed on a conspicuous throne of thorns,
Grasping an iron sceptre, and immured
Within a splendid prison, whose stern bounds
Shut him from all that's good or dear on earth,
His soul asserts not its humanity?

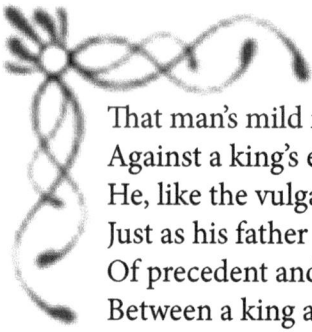

That man's mild nature rises not in war
Against a king's employ? No—'tis not strange.
He, like the vulgar, thinks, feels, acts and lives
Just as his father did; the unconquered powers
Of precedent and custom interpose
Between a king and virtue. Stranger yet,
To those who know not nature, nor deduce
The future from the present, it may seem,
That not one slave, who suffers from the crimes
Of this unnatural being ; not one wretch,
Whose children famish, and whose nuptial bed
In earth's unpitying bosom, rears an arm
To dash him from his throne!

                    Those gilded flies
That, basking in the sunshine of a court,
Fatten on its corruption !—what are they?
—The drones of the community; they feed
On the mechanic's labour: the starved hind
For them compels the stubborn glebe to yield
Its unshared harvests; and yon squalid form,
Leaner than fleshless misery, that wastes
A sunless life in the unwholesome mine,
Drags out in labour a protracted death,
To glut their grandeur; many faint with toil,
That few may know the cares and woe of sloth.

Whence, thinkest thou, kings and parasites arose?
Whence that unnatural line of drones, who heap
Toil and unvanquishable penury
On those who build their palaces, and bring
Their daily bread ?—From vice, black loathsome vice;
From rapine, madness, treachery, and wrong;
From all that genders misery, and makes
Of earth this thorny wilderness; from lust,
Revenge, and murder......And when reason's voice,
Loud as the voice of nature, shall have waked

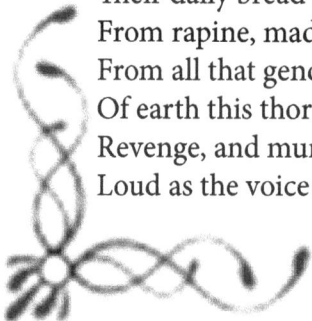

The nations; and mankind perceive that vice
Is discord, war, and misery; that virtue
Is peace, and happiness, and harmony;
When man's maturer nature shall disdain
The playthings of its childhood ;—kingly glare
Will lose its power to dazzle; its authority
Will silently pass by; the gorgeous throne
Shall stand unnoticed in the regal hall,
Fast falling to decay; whilst falsehood's trade
Shall be as hateful and unprofitable
As that of truth is now.

               Where is the fame
Which the vaiu-glorious mighty of the earth
Seek to eternize? Oh! the faintest sound
From time's light footfall, the minutest wave
That swells the flood of ages, whelms in nothing
The unsubstantial bubble. Aye! to-day
Stern is the tyrant's mandate, red the gaze
That flashes desolation, strong the arm
That scatters multitudes. To-morrow comes!
That mandate is a thunder-peal that died
In ages past; that gaze, a transient flash
On which the midnight closed, and on that arm
The worm has made his meal.

               The virtuous man,
Who, great in his humility, as kings
Are little in their grandeur; he who leads
Invincibly a life of resolute good,
And stands amid the silent dungeon-depths
More free and fearless than the trembling judge,
Who, clothed in venal power, vainly strove
To bind the impassive spirit;—when he falls,
His mild eye beams benevolence no more:
Withered the hand outstretched but to relieve;
Sunk reason's simple eloquence that rolled

31

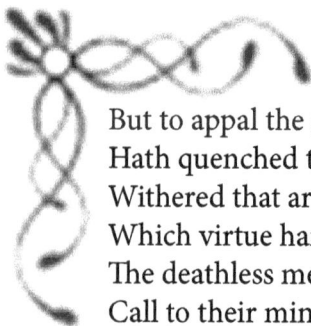

But to appal the guilty. Yes! the grave
Hath quenched that eye, and death's relentless frost
Withered that arm: but the unfading fame
Which virtue hangs upon its votary's tomb;
The deathless memory of that man, whom kings
Call to their mind and tremble; the remembrance
With which the happy spirit contemplates
Its well-spent pilgrimage on earth,
Shall never pass away.

Nature rejects the monarch, not the man;
The subject not the citizen: for kings
And subjects, mutual foes, for ever play
A losing game into each other's hands,
Whose stakes are vice and misery. The man
Of virtuous soul commands not, nor obeys.
Power, like a desolating pestilence,
Pollutes whate'er it touches; and obedience,
Bane of all genius, virtue, freedom, truth,
Makes slaves of men, and, of the human frame,
A mechanized automaton.

                    When Nero,
High over flaming Rome, with savage joy
Lowered like a fiend, drank with enraptured ear
The shrieks of agonizing death, beheld
The frightful desolation spread, and felt
A new created sense within his soul
Thrill to the sight, and vibrate to the sound;
Thinkest thou his grandeur had not overcome

The force of human kindness? and, when Rome,
With one stern blow, hurled not the tyrant down,
Crushed not the arm red with her dearest blood,
Had not submissive abjectness destroyed
Nature's suggestions?

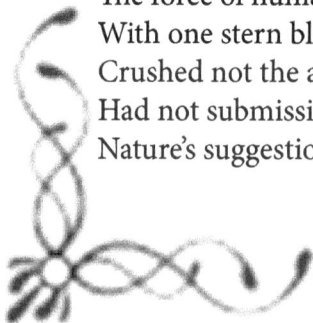

32

Look on yonder earth:
The golden harvests spring ; the unfailing sun
Sheds light a:nd life; the fruits, the flowers, the trees,
Arise in due succession; all things speak
Peace, harmony, and love. The universe,
In nature's silent eloquence, declares
That all fulfil the works of love and joy,—
All but the outcast man. He fabricates
The sword which stabs his peace; he cherisheth
The snakes that gnaw his heart; he raiseth up
The tyrant, whose delight is in his woe,
Whose sport is in his agony. Yon sun,
Lights it the great alone? You silver beams,
Sleep they less sweetly on the cottage thatch,
Thai1 on the dome of kings? Is mother earth
A step-dame to her numerous sons, who earn
Her unshared gifts with unremitting toil;
A mother only to those puling babes
Who, nursed in ease and luxury, make men
The playthings of their babyhood, and mar,
In self-important childishness, that peace
Which men alone appreciate?

      Spirit of Nature! no.
The pure diffusion of thy essence throbs
Alike in every human heart.
      Thou, aye, erectest there
Thy throne of power unappealable
Thou art the judge beneath whose nod
Man's brief and frail authority
      Is powerless as the wind
      That passeth idly by.
Thine the tribunal which surpasseth
  The shew of human justice,
      As God surpasses man.

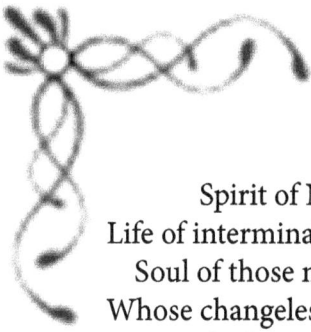

Spirit of Nature! thou
Life of interminable multitudes;
Soul of those mighty spheres
Whose changeless paths thro' Heaven's deep silence lie;
Soul of that smallest being,
The dwelling of whose life
Is one faint April sun-gleam;—
Man, like these passive things,
Thy will unconsciously fulfilleth:
Like theirs, his age of endless peace,
Which time is fast maturing,
Will swiftly, surely come;
And the unbounded frame, which thou pervadest,
Will be without a flaw
Marring its perfect symmetry.

IV

How beautiful this night! the balmiest sigh,
Which vernal zephyrs breathe in evening's ear,
Were discord to the speaking quietude
That wraps this moveless scene. Heaven's ebon vault,
Studded with stars unutterably bright,
Through which the moon's unclouded grandeur rolls,
Seems like a canopy which love had spread
To curtain her sleeping world. Yon gentle hills,
Robed in a garment of untrodden Snow;
Yon darksome rocks, whence icicles depend,
So stainless, that their white and glittering spires
Tinge not the moon's pure beam; yon castled steep,
Whose banner hangeth o'er the time-worn tower
So idly, that rapt fancy deemeth it
A metaphor of peace;—all form a scene
Where musing solitude might love to lift
Her soul above this sphere of earthliness;
Where silence undisturbed might watch alone,
So cold, so bright, so still.

        The orb of day,
In southern climes, o'er ocean's waveless field
Sinks sweetly smiling: not the faintest breath
Steals o'er the unruffled deep; the clouds of eve
Reflect unmoved the lingering beam of day;
And vesper's image on the western main
Is beautifully still. To-morrow comes:
Cloud upon cloud, in dark and deepening mass,
Roll o'er the blackened waters; the deep roar
Of distant thunder mutters awfully;
Tempest unfolds its pinion o'er the gloom
That shrouds the boiling surge; the pityless fiend,
With all his winds and lightnings, tracks his prey;

Ah! whence yon glare
That fires the arch of heaven?—that dark red smoke
Blotting the silver moon? The stars are quenched
In darkness, and the pure and spangling snow
Gleams faintly through the gloom that gathers round!
Hark to that roar, whose swift and deafening peals
In countless echoes through the mountains ring,
Startling pale midnight on her starry throne!
Now swells the intermingling din; the jar
Frequent and frightful of the bursting bomb;
The falling beam, the shriek, the groan, the shout,
The ceaseless clangour, and the rush of men
Inebriate with rage:—loud, and more loud
The discord grows; till pale death shuts the scene,
And o'er the conqueror and the conquered draws
His cold and bloody shroud.—Of all the men
Whom day's departing beam saw blooming there,
In proud and vigorous health; of all the hearts
That beat with anxious life at sun-set there;
How few survive, how few are beating now!
All is deep silence, like the fearful calm
That slumbers in the storms portentous pause;
Save when the frantic wail of widowed love
Comes shuddering on the blast, or the faint moan
With which some soul bursts from the frame of clay
Wrapt round its struggling powers.

                    The grey morn
Dawns on the mournful scene; the sulphurous smoke
Before the icy wind slow rolls away,
And the bright beams of frosty morning dance
Along the spangling snow. There tracks of blood
Even to the forest's depth, and scatter'd arms,
And lifeless warriors, whose hard lineaments
Death's self could change not, mark the dreadful path

36

Death's self could change not, mark the dreadful **path**
Of the outsallying victors: far behind,
Black ashes note where their proud city stood.
Within you forest is a gloomy glen—
Eachtree which guards its darkness from the day,
Waves o'er a warrior's tomb.

                I see thee shrink,
Surpassing Spirit!—wert thou human else?
I see a shade of doubt and horror fleet
Across thy stainless features: yet fear not;
This is no unconnected misery,
Nor stands uncaused, and irretrievable.
Man's evil nature, that apology
Which kings who rule, and cowards who crouch, set up
For their unnumbered crimes, sheds not the blood
Which desolates the discord-wasted land.
From kings, and priests, and statesmen, war arose,
Whose safety is man's deep unbettered woe,
Whose grandeur his debasement. Let the axe
Strike at the root, the poison-tree will fall;
And where its venomed exhalations spread
Ruin, and death, and woe, where millions lay
Quenching the serpent's famine, and their bones
Bleaching unburied in the putrid blast,
A garden shall arise, in loveliness
Surpassing fabled Eden.

                Hath Nature's soul,
That formed this world so beautiful, that spread
Earth's lap with plenty, and life's smallest chord
Strung to unchanging unison, that gave
The happy birds their dwelling in the grove,
That yielded to the wanderers of the deep
The lovely silence of the unfathomed main,

Nature!—no!
Kings, priests, and statesmen, blast the human flower
Even in its tender bud; their influence darts
Like subtle poison through the bloodless veins
Of desolate society. The child,
Ere he can lisp his mother's sacred name,
Swells with the unnatural pride of crime, and lifts
His baby-sword even in a hero's mood.
This infant-arm becomes the bloodiest scourge
Of devastated earth; whilst specious names,
Learnt in soft childhood's unsuspecting hour,
Serve as the sophisms with which manhood dims
Bright reason's ray, and sanctifies the sword
Upraised to shed a brother's innocent blood.
Let priest-led slaves cease to proclaim that man
Inherits vice and misery, when force
And falsehood hang even o'er the cradled babe,
Stifling with rudest grasp all natural good.

Ah! to the stranger-soul, when first it peeps
From its new tenement, and looks abroad
For happiness and sympathy, how stern
And desolate a tract is this wide world!
How withered all the buds of natural good!
No shade, no shelter from the sweeping storms
Of pityless power! On its wretched frame,
Poisoned, perchance, by the disease and woe
Heaped on the wretched parent whence it sprung
By morals, law, and custom, the pure winds
Of heaven, that renovate the insect tribes,
May breathe not. The untainting light of day
May visit not its longings. It is bound
Ere it has life: yea, all the chains are forged
Long ere its being: all liberty and love
And peace is torn from its defencelessness;

Cursed from its birth, even from its cradle doomed
To abjectness and bondage!

Throughout this varied and eternal world
Soul is the only element, the block
That for uncounted ages has remained.
The moveless pillar of a mountain's weight
Is active, living spirit. Every grain
Is sentient both in unity and part,
And the minutest atom comprehends
A world of loves and hatreds; these beget
Evil and good: hence truth, and falsehood spring;
Hence will, and thought, and action, all the germs
Of pain or pleasure, sympathy or hate,
That variegate the eternal universe.
Soul is not more polluted than the beams
Of heaven's pure orb, ere round their rapid lines
The taint of earth-born atmospheres arise.
Man is of soul and body, formed for deeds
Of high resolve, on fancy's boldest wing
To soar unwearied, fearlessly to turn
The keenest pangs to peacefulness, and taste
The joys which mingled sense and spirit yield.
Or he is formed for abjectness and woe,
To grovel on the dunghill of his fears,
To shrink at every sound, to quench the flame
Of natural love in sensualism, to know
That hour as blest when on his worthless days
The frozen hand of death shall set its seal,
Yet fear the cure, though hating the disease.
The one is man that shall hereafter be;
The other, man as vice has made him now.

War is the statesman's game, the priest's delight,
The lawyer's jest, the hired assassin's trade,

And, to those royal murderers, whose mean thrones
Are bought by crimes of treachery and gore,
The bread they eat, the staff on which they lean.
Guards, garbed in blood-red livery, surround
Their palaces, participate the crimes
That force defends, and from a nation's rage
Secures the crown, which all the curses reach
That famine, frenzy, woe, and penury breathe.
These are the hired bravos who defend
The tyrant's throne—the bullies of his fear:
These are the sinks and channels of worst vice,
The refuse of society, the dregs
Of all that is most vile: their cold hearts blend
Deceit with sternness, ignorance with pride,
All that is mean and villainous, with rage
Which hopelessness of good, and self-contempt,
Alone might kindle; they are decked in wealth,
Honour and power, then are sent abroad
To do their work. The pestilence that stalks
In gloomy triumph through some eastern land
Is less destroying. They cajole with gold,
And promises of fame, the thoughtless youth
Already crushed with servitude: he knows
His wretchedness too late, and cherishes
Repentance for his ruin, when his doom
Is sealed in gold and blood!
Those too the tyrant serve, who, skilled to snare
The feet of justice in the toils of law,
Stand, ready to oppress the weaker still;
And, right or wrong, will vindicate for gold,
Sneering at public virtue, which beneath
Their pityless tread lies torn and trampled, where
Honour sits smiling at the sale of truth.

Then grave and hoary-headed hypocrites,

40

Without a hope, a passion, or a love,
Who, through a life of luxury and lies,
Have crept by flattery to the seats of power,
Support the system whence their honours flow....
They have three words:—well tyrants know their use,
Well pay them for the loan, with usury
Torn from a bleeding world!— —, Hell, and Heaven.
A vengeful, pityless,——and fiend,
Whose mercy is a nick-name for the rage
Of tameless tygers hungering for blood.
Hell, a red gulf of everlasting fire,
Where poisonous and undying worms prolong
Eternal misery to those hapless slaves
Whose life has been a penance for its crimes.
And Heaven, a meed for those who dare belie
Their human nature, quake, believe, and cringe
Before the mockeries of earthly power.

These tools the tyrant tempers to his work,
Wields in his wrath, and as he wills destroys,
Omnipotent in wickedness: the while
Youth springs, age moulders, manhood tamely does
His bidding, bribed by short-lived joys to lend
Force to the weakness of his trembling arm.

They rise, they fall; one generation comes
Yielding its harvest to destruction's scythe.
It fades, another blossoms, yet behold!
Red glows the tyrant's stamp-mark on its bloom,
Withering and cankering deep its passive prime.
He has invented lying words and modes,
Empty and vain as his own coreless heart;
Evasive meani: gs, nothings of much sound,
To lure the heedless victim to the toils
Spread round the valley of its paradise.

Look to thyself, priest, conqueror, or prince!
Whether thy trade is fal,ehood, and thy lusts
Deep wallow in the earnings of the poor,
With whom thy master was :or thou delightst
In numbering o'er the myriads of thy slain,
All misery weighing nothing in the scale
Against thy short-lived fame: or thou
VVith cowardice and crime the groanindgo lsatn ldo, ad
A pomp-fed king. Look to thy wretched self!
Aye, art thou not the veriest slave that e'er
Crawled on the loathing earth? Are not thy days
Days of unsatisfying listlessness?
Dost thou not cry, ere night's long rack is o'er,
When will the morning come? Is not thy youth
A vain and feverish dream of sensualism?
Thy manhood blighted with unripe disease?
Are not thy views of unregretted death
Drear, comfortless, and horrible? Thy mind
Is it not morbid as thy nerveless frame,
Incapable of judgment, hope, or love?
And dost thou wish the errors to survive
That bar thee from all sympathies of good,
After the miserable interest
Thou holdst in their protraction? When the grave
Has swallowed up thy memory and thyself,
Dost thou desire the bane that poisons earth
To twine its roots around thy coffined clay,
Spring from thy bones, and blossom on thy tomb,
That of its fruit thy babes may eat and die?

V

Thus do the generations of the earth
Go to the grave, and issue from the womb,
Surviving still the imperishable change
That renovates the world; even as the leaves
Which the keen frost-wind of the waning year
Has scattered on the forest soil, and heaped
For many seasons there, though long they choke,
Loading with loathsome rottenness the land,
All germs of promise. Yet when the tall trees
From which they fell, shorn of their lovely shapes,
Lie level with the earth to moulder there,
They fertilize the land they long deformed,
Till from the breathing lawn a forest springs
Of youth, integrity, and loveliness,
Like that which gave it life, to spring and die.
Thus suicidal selfishness, that blights
The fairest feelings of the opening heart,
Is destined to decay, whilst from the soil
Shall spring all virtue, all delight, all love,
And judgment cease to wage
unnatural war With passion's unsubduable array.

Twin-sister of religion, selfishness!
Rival in crime and falsehood, aping all
Commerce has set the mark of selfishness,
The signet of its all-enslaving power
Upon a shining ore, and called it gold:
Before whose image bow the vulgar great,
The vainly rich, the miserable proud,
The mob of peasants, nobles, priests, and kings,
And with blind feelings reverence the power
That grinds them to the dust of misery.
But in the temple of their hireling hearts

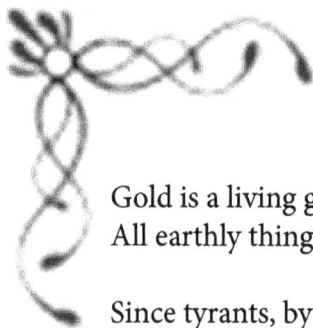

Gold is a living god, and rules in scorn
All earthly things but virtue.

Since tyrants, by the sale of human life,
Heap luxuries to their sensualism, and fame
To their wide-wasting and insatiate pride,
Success has sanctioned to a credulous world
The ruin, the disgrace, the woe of war.
His hosts of blind and unresisting dupes
The despot numbers; from his cabinet
These puppets of his schemes he moves at will,
Even as the slaves by force or famine driven,
Beneath a vulgar master, to perform
A task of cold and brutal di udgery;—
Hardened to hope, insensible to fear,
Scarce living pullies of a dead machine,
Mere wheels of work and articles of trade,
That grace the proud and noisy pomp of wealth!

The harmony and happiness of man
Yields to the wealth of nations; that which lifts
His nature to the heaven of its pride,
Is bartered for the poison of his soul;
The weight that drags to earth his towering hopes,
Blighting all prospect but of selfish gain,
Withering all passion but of slavish fear,
Extinguishing all free and generous love
Of enterprize and daring, even the pulse
That fancy kindles in the beating heart
To mingle with sensation, it destroys,—
Leaves nothing but the sordid lust of self,
The groveling hope of interest and gold,
Unqualified, unmingled, unredeemed
Even by hypocrisy.

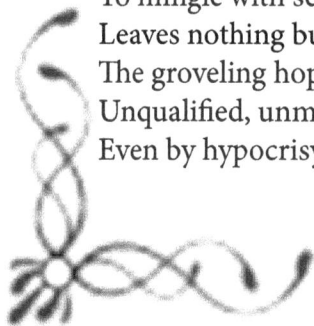

And statesmen boast
Of wealth! The wordy eloquence that lives
A ftert he ruin of their hearts, can gild
The bitter poison of a nation's woe,
Can turn the worship of the servile mob
To their corrupt and glaring idol fame,
From virtue, trampled by its iron tread,
Although its dazzling pedestal be raised
Amid the horrors of a limb-strewn field,
With desolated dwellings smoking round.
The man of ease, who, by his warm fire-side,
To deeds of charitable intercourse
And bare fulfilment of the common laws
Of decency and prejudice, confines
The struggling nature of his human heart,
Is duped by their cold sophistry; he sheds
A passing tear perchance upon the wreck
How many a vulgar Cato has compelled•
His energies, no longer tameless then,
To mould a pin, or fabricate a nail!
How many a Newton, to whose passive ken
Those mighty spheres that gem infinity
Were only specks of tinsel, fixed in heaven
To light the midnights of his native town!

Yet every heart contains perfection's germ:
The wisest of the sages of the earth,
That ever from the stores of reason drew
Science and truth, and virtue's dreadless tone,
Were but a weak and inexperienced boy,
Proud, sensual, unimpassioned, unimbued
With pure desire and universal love,
Compared to that high being, of cloudless brain,
Untainted passion, elevated will,
Which death (who even would linger long in awe

Within his noble presence, and beneath
His changeless eyebeam,) might alone subdue.
Him, every slave now dragging through the filth
Of some corrupted city his sad life,
Pining with famine, swoln with luxury,
Blunting the keenness of his spiritual sense
With narrow schemings and unworthy cares,
Or madly rushing through all violent crime,
To move the deep stagnation of his soul,—
Might imitate and equal.

                 But mean lust
Has bound its chains so tight around the earth,
Unalterable will, quenchless desire
Of universal happiness, the heart
That beats with it in unison, the brain,
Whose ever wakeful wisdom toils to change
Reason's rich stores for its eternal weal.

This commerce of sincerest virtue needs
No mediative signs of selfishness,
No jealous intercourse of wretched gain,
No balancings of prudence, cold and long;
In just and equal measure all is weighed,
One scale contains the sum of human weal,
And one, the good man's heart.

                 How vainly seek
The selfish for that happiness denied
To aught but virtue! Blind and hardened, they,
Who hope for peace amid the storms of care,
Who covet power they know not how to use,
And sigh for pleasure they refuse to give,—
Madly they frustrate still their own designs;
And, where they hope that quiet to enjoy

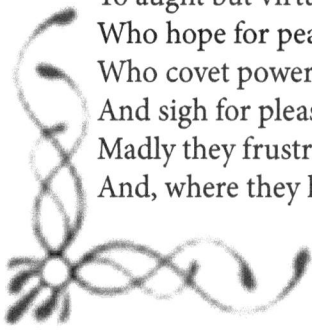

Which virtue pictures, bitterness of soul,
Pining regrets, and vain repentances,
Disease, disgust, and lassitude, pervade
Their valueless and miserable lives.

But hoary-headed selfishness has felt
Its death-blow, and is tottering to the grave:
A brighter morn awaits the human day,
When every transfer of earth's natural gifts
Shall be a commerce of good words and works;
When poverty and wealth, the thirst of fame,
The fear of infamy, disease, and woe,
War with its million horrors, and fierce hell
Shall live but in the memory of time,
Who, like a penitent libertine, shall start,
Look back, and shudder at his younger years.

VI

All touch, all eye, all ear,
The Spirit felt the Fairy's burning speech.
　　O'er the thin texture of its frame,
The varying periods painted changing glows,
　　　　As on a summer even,
When soul-enfolding music floats around,
　　The stainless mirror of the lake
　　Re-images the eastern gloom,
Mingling convulsively its purple hues
　　　　With sunset's burnished gold.

　　　Then thus the Spirit spoke:
It is a wild and miserable world!
　　　Thorny, and full of care,
Which every fiend can make his prey at will.
　　O Fairy! in the lapse of years,
　　　　Is there no hope in store?
　　　　Will you vast suns roll on
Interminably, still illuming
The night of so many wretched souls,
　　　And see no hope for them?
Will not the universal Spirit e'er
Revivify this withered limb of Heaven?

　　　The Fairy calmly smiled
In comfort, and a kindling gleam of hope
　　Suffdsed the Spirits lineaments.
Oh! rest thee tranquil; chase those fearful doubts,
Which ne'er could rack an everlasting soul,
That sees the chains which bind it to its doom.
Yes! crime and misery are in yonder earth,
　　　Falsehood, mistake, and lust;
　　　But the eternal world

49

Contains at once the evil and the cure.
Some eminent in virtue shall start up,
        Even in perversest time:
The truths of their pure lips, that never die,
Shall bind the scorpion falsehood with a wreath
        Of ever-living flame,
Until the monster sting itself to death.
    How sweet a scene will earth become!
Of purest spirits, a pure dwelling-place,
Symphonious with the planetary spheres,
When man, with changeless nature coalescing,
Will undertake regeneration's work,
When its ungenial poles no longer point
        To the red and baleful sun
        That faintly twinkles there.

        Spirit! on yonder earth,
    Falsebpod now triumphs; deadly power
Has fixed its seal upon the lip of truth!
    Madness and misery are there!
The happiest is most wretched! yet confide,
Until pure health-drops from the cup of joy,
Fall like a dew of balm upon the world.
Now, to the scene I shew, in silence turn,
And read the blood-stained charter of all woe,
Which nature soon, with recreating hand,
Will blot in mercy from the book of earth.
How bold the flight of passion's wandering wing,
How swift the step of reason's firmer tread,
How calm and sweet the victories of life,
How terrorless the triumph of the grave!
How powerless were the mightiest monarch's arm,
Vain his loud threat, and impotent his frown!
How ludicrous the priest's dogmatic roar!
The weight of his exterminating curse,

R——! but for thee, prolific fiend,
Who peoplest earth with demons, hell with men,
And heaven with slaves!

Thou taintest all thou lookest upon !—the stars,
Which on thy cradle beamed so brightly sweet,
Were gods to the distempered playfulness
Of thy untutored infancy: the trees,
The grass, the clouds, the mountains, and the sea,
All living things that walk, swim, creep, or fly,
VITere gods: the sun had homage, and the moon
Her worshipper. Then thou becamest, a boy,
More daring in thy frenzies: every shape,
Monstrous or vast, or beautifully wild,
Which, from sensation's relics, fancy culls;

The spirits of the air, the shuddering ghost,
The genii of the elements, the powers
That give a shape to nature's varied works,
Had ,life and place in the corrupt belief
Of thy blind heart: yet still thy youthful hands
Were pure of human blood. Then manhood gave
Its strength and ardour to thy frenzied brain;
Thine eager gaze scanned the stupendous scene
Whose wonders mocked the knowledge of thy pride:
Their everlasting and unchanging laws
Reproached thine ignorance. Awhile thou stoodst
Baffled and gloomy; then thou didst sum up
The elements of all that thou didst know;
The changing seasons, winter's leafless reign,
The budding of the heaven-breathing trees,
The eternal orbs that beautify the night,
The sun-rise, and the setting of the moon,
Earthquakes and wars, and poisons and disease,
And all their causes, to an abstract point,

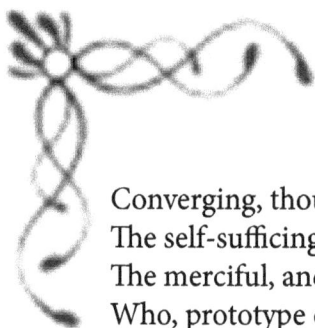

Converging, thou didst bend, and called it—God!
The self-sufficing, the omnipotent,
The merciful, and the avenging God!
Who, prototype of human misrule, sits
High in heaven's realm, upon a golden throne,
Even like an earthly king; and whose dread work,
Hell   —   —   —   —

—   —   —   —   —

—   —   —   —   —

Earth heard the name; earth trembled, as the smoke
Of his revenge ascended up to heaven,
Blotting the constellations; and the cries
Of millions, butchered in sweet confidence
And unsuspecting peace, even when the bonds
Of safety were confirmed by wordy oaths
Sworn in his dreadful name, rung through the land;
Whilst innocent babes writhed on thy stubborn spear,
And thou didst laugh to hear the mother's shriek
Of maniac gladness, as the sacred steel
Felt cold in her torn entrails!

Religion! thou wert then in manhood's prime:
But age crept on: one God would not suffice
For senile puerility; thou framedst
A tale to suit thy dotage, and to glut
Thy misery-thirsting soul, that the mad fiend
Thy wickedness had pictured, might afford
A plea for sating the unnatural thirst
For murder, rapine, violence, and crime,
That still consumed thy being, even when
Thou heardest the step of fate ,—that flames might ugh
Thy funeral scene, and the shrill horrent shrieks
Of parents dying on the pile that burned
To light their children to thy paths, the roar
Of the encircling flames, the exulting cries

Of thine apostles, loud commingling there,
    Might sate thine hungry ear
    Even on the bed of death!

But now contempt is mocking thy grey hairs;
Thou art descending to the darksome grave,
Unhonoured and unpitied, but by those
Whose pride is passing by like thine, and sheds,
Like thine, a glare that fades before the sun
Of truth, and shines but in the dreadful night
That long has lowered above the ruined world.

Throughout these infinite orbs of mingling light,
Of which yon earth is one, is wide diffused
A spirit of activity and life,
That knows no term, cessation, or decay;
That fades not when the lamp of earthly life,
Extinguished in the dampness of the grave,
Awhile there slumbers, more than when the babe
In the dim newness of its being feels
The impulses of sublunary things,
And all is wonder to unpractised sense:
But, active, stedfast, and eternal, still
Guides the fierce whirlwind, in the tempest roars,
Cheers in the day, breathes in the balmy groves,
Strengthens in health, and poisons in disease;
And in the storm of change, that ceaselessly
Rolls round the eternal universe, and shakes
Its undecaying battlement, presides,
Apportioning with irresistible law
The place each spring of its machine shall fill;
So that when waves on waves tumultuous heap
Confusion to the clouds, and fiercely driven
Heaven's lightnings scorch the uprooted ocean-fords,
Whilst, to the eye of shipwrecked mariner,

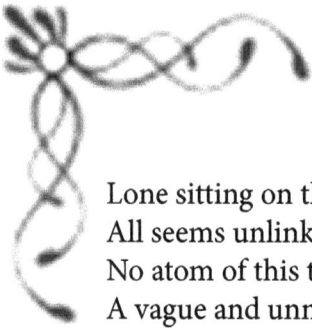

Lone sitting on the bare and shuddering rock,
All seems unlinked contingency and chance:
No atom of this turbulence fulfils
A vague and unnecessitated task,
Or acts but as it must and ought to act.
Even the minutest molecule of light,
That in an April sun-beam's fleeting glow
Fulfills its destined, though invisible work,
The universal Spirit guides; nor less,
When merciless ambition, or mad zeal,
Has led two hosts of dupes to battle-field,
That, blind, they there may dig each other's graves,
And call the sad work—glory, does it rule
All passions: not a thought, a will, an act,
No working of the tyrant's moody mind,
Nor one misgiving of the slaves who boast
Their servitude, to hide the shame they feel,
Nor the events enchaining every will,
That from the depths of unrecorded time
Have drawn all-influencing virtue, pass
Unrecognized, or unforeseen by thee,
Soul of the Universe! eternal spring
Of life and death, of happiness and woe,
Of all that chequers the phantasmal scene
That floats before our eyes in wavering light,
Which gleams but on the darkness of our prison,
      Whose chains and massy walls
      We feel, but cannot see.

Spirit of Nature! all-sufficing Power,
Necessity! thou mother of the world!
Unlike the God of human error, thou
Requirest no prayers or praises; the caprice
Of man's weak will belongs no more to thee
Than do the changeful passions of his breast

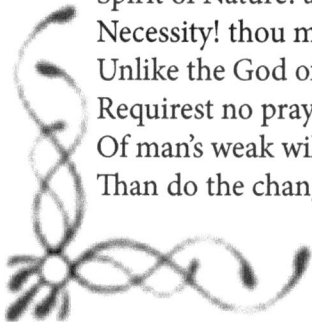

To thy unvarying harmony: the slave,
Whose horrible lusts spread misery o'er the world,
And the good man, who lifts, with virtuous pride,
His being, in the sight of happiness,
That springs from his own works ; the poison-tree,
Beneath whose shade all life is withered up,
And the fair oak, whose leafy dome affords
A temple where the vows of happy love
Are registered, are equal in thy sight:
No love, no hate thou cherishest; revenge
And favoritism, and worst desire of fame
Thou knowest not: all that the wide world contains
Are but thy passive instruments, and thou
Regardst them all with an impartial eye,
Whose joy or pain thy nature cannot feel,
   Because thou hast not human sense,
   Because thou art not human mind.

   Yes! when the sweeping storm of time
Has sung its death-dirge o'er the ruined fanes
And broken altars of the almighty fiend,
Whose name usurps thy honours, and the blood
Through centuries clotted there, has floated down
The tainted flood of ages, shalt thou live
Unchangeable! A shrine is raised to thee,
   Which, nor the tempest-breath of time,
   Nor the interminable flood,
   Over earth's slight pageant rolling,
      Availeth to destroy,—
The sensitive extension of the world.
   That wonderous and eternal fane,
Where pain and pleasure, good and evil join,
To do the will of strong necessity,
   And life, in multitudinous shapes,
Still pressing forward where no term can be,

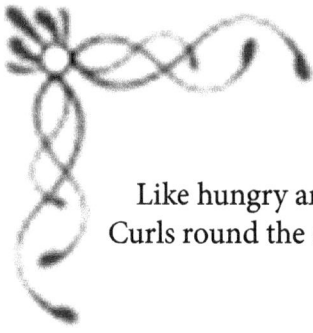

Like hungry and unresisting flame
Curls round the eternal columns of its strength.

VII

SPIRIT

I was an infant when my mother went
To see an atheist burned. She took me there:
The dark-robed priests were met around the pile;
The multitude was gazing silently;
And as the culprit passed with dauntless mien,
Tempered disdain in his unaltering eye,
Mixed with a quiet smile, shone calmly forth:
The thirsty fire crept round his manly limbs;
His resolute eyes were scorched to blindness soon;
His death-pang rent my heart! the insensate mob
Uttered a cry of triumph, and I wept.
Weep not, child ! cried my mother, for that man
Has said, There is no God.

FAIRY.

There is no God!
Nature confirms the faith his death-groan sealed:
Let heaven and earth, let man's revolving race,
His ceaseless generations tell their tale;
Let every part depending on the chain
That links it to the whole, point to the hand
That grasps its term! let every seed that falls
        O Spirit! through the sense
By which thy inner nature was apprised
   Of outward shevvs, vague dreams have rolled,
   And varied reminiscences have waked
        Tablets that never fade;
All things have been imprinted there,
The stars, the sea, the earth, the sky,
Even the unshapeliest lineaments
   Of wild and fleeting visions

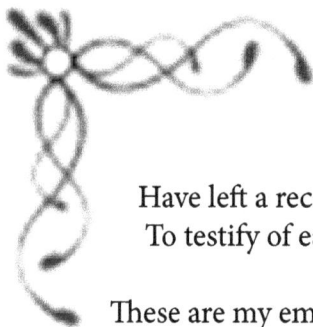

Have left a record there
To testify of earth.

These are my empire, for to me is given
The wonders of the human world to keep,
And fancy's thin creations to endow
With manner, being, and reality;
Therefore a wondrous phantom, from the dreams
Of human errors dense and purblind faith,
I will evoke, to meet thy questioning.
Ahasuerus, rise!

A strange and woe-worn wight
Arose beside the battlement,
And stood unmoving there.
His inessential figure cast no shade
Upon the golden floor;
His port and mien bore mark of many years,
And chronicles of untold ancientness
Were legible within his beamless eye:
Yet his cheek bore the mark of youth;
Freshness and vigour knit his manly frame;
The wisdom of old age was mingled there
With youth's primTval dauntlessness;
And inexpressible woe,
Chastened by fearless resignation, gave
An awful grace to his all-speaking brow.

SPIRIT.

Is there a God?

AHASUERUS.

Is there a God ?—aye, an almighty God,
And vengeful as almighty! Once his voice
Was heard on earth: earth shuddered at the sound;
The fiery-visaged firmament expressed
Abhorrence, and the grave of nature yawned
To swallow all the dauntless and the good
That dared to hurl defiance at his throne,
Girt as it was with power. None but slaves
Survived,—cold-blooded slaves, who did the work
Of tyrannous omnipotence; whose souls
No honest indignation ever urged
To elevated daring, to one deed
Which gross and sensual self did not pollute.
These slaves built temples for the omnipotent,
Gorgeous and vast: the costly altars smoked
With human blood, and hideous pTans rung
Through all the long-drawn aisles. A murderer heard
His voice in Egypt, one whose gifts and arts
Had raised him to his eminence in power,
Accomplice of — — — in crime,
And confidant of the all-knowing one.
        These were Jehovah's words.

From an eternity of idleness
I, God, awoke; in seven days' toil made earth
From nothing; rested, and created man:
I placed him in a paradise, and there
Planted the tree of evil, so that he
Might eat and perish, and my soul procure
Wherewith to sate its malice, and to turn,
Even like a heartless conqueror of the earth,
All misery to my fame. The race of men
Chosen to my honour, with impunity

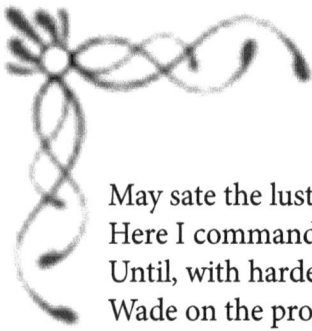

May sate the lusts I planted in their heart.
Here I command thee hence to lead them on,
Until, with hardened feet, their conquering troops
Wade on the promised soil through woman's blood,
And make my name be dreaded through the laud.
Yet ever burning flame and ceaseless woe
Shall be the doom of their eternal souls,
With every soul on this ungrateful earth,
Virtuous or vicious, weak or strong,—even all
Shall perish, to fulfil the blind revenge
(Which you, to men, call justice) of their God.

      The murderer's brow
Quivered with horror.

      God omnipotent,
Is there no mercy? must our punishment
Be endless? will long ages roll away,
And see no term? Oh ! wherefore hast thou made
In mockery and wrath this evil earth?
Mercy becomes the powerful—be but just:
0 God! repent and save.

One way remains:
I will beget a son, and he shall bear
The sins of all the world ; he shall arise
In an unnoticed corner of the earth,
And there shall die upon a cross, and purge
The universal crime; so that the few
On whom my grace descends, those who are marked
As vessels to the honour of their God,
May credit this strange sacrifice, and save
Their souls alive: millions shall live and die,
Who ne'er shall call upon their Saviour's name,
But, unredeemed, go to the gaping grave.

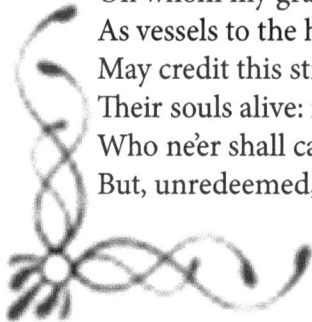

Thousands shall deem it an old woman's tale,
Such as the nurses frighten babes withal:
These, in a gulph of anguish and of flame,
Shall curse their reprobation endlessly,
Yet tenfold pangs shall force them to avow,
Even on their beds of torment, where they howl,
My honour, and the justice of their doom.
What then avail their virtuous deeds, their thoughts
Of purity, with radiant genius bright,
Or lit with human reason's earthly ray?
Many are called, but few will I elect.
Do thou my bidding, Moses!
When I awoke hell burned within my brain,
Which staggered on its seat; for all around
The mouldering relics of my kindred lay,
Even as the Almighty's ire arrested them,
And in their various attitudes of death
My murdered children's mute and eyeless sculls
Glared ghastily upon me.

                    But my soul,
From sight and sense of the polluting woe
Of tyranny, had long learned to prefer
Hell's freedom to the servitude of heaven.
Therefore I rose, and dauntlessly began
My lonely and unending pilgrimage,
Resolved to wage unweariable war
With my almighty tyrant, and to hurl
Defiance at his impotence to harm
Beyond the curse I bore. The very hand
That barred my passage to the peaceful grave
Has crushed the earth to misery, and given
Its empire to the chosen of his slaves.
These have I seen, even from the earliest dawn
Of weak, unstable, and precarious power;

Then preaching peace, as now they practise war,
So, when they turned but from the massacre
Of unoffending infidels, to quench
Their thirst for ruin in the very blood
That flowed in their own veins, and pityless zeal
Froze every human feeling, as the wife
Sheathed in her husband's heart the sacred steel,
Even whilst its hopes were dreaming of her love;
And friends to friends, brothers to brothers stood
Opposed in bloodiest battle-field, and war,
Scarce satiable by fate's last death-draught waged,
Drunk from the wine-press of the Almighty's wrath;
Whilst the red cross in mockery of peace,
Pointed to victory! When the fray was done,
No remnant of the exterminated faith
Survived to tell its ruin, but the flesh,
With putrid smoke poisoning the atmosphere,
That rotted on the half-extinguished pile.

Yes! I have seen God's worshippers unsheathe
The sword of his revenge, when grace descended,
Confirming all unnatural impulses,
To sanctify their desolating deeds;
And frantic priests waved the ill-omened cross
O'er the unhappy earth: then shone the Sun
On showers of gore from the upflashing steel
Of safe assassination, and all crime
Made stingless by the spirits of the Lord,
And blood-red rainbows canopied the land.
Spirit! no year of my eventful being
Has passed unstained by crime and misery,
Which flows from God's own faith. I've marked his
        slaves
With tongues whose lies are venomous, beguile
The insensate mob, and whilst one hand was red

With murder, feign to stretch the other out
For brotherhood and peace; and that they now
Babble of love and mercy, whilst their deeds
Are marked with all the narrowness and crime
That freedom's young arm dare not yet chastise;
Reason may claim our gratitude, who now
Establishing the imperishable throne
Of truth, and stubborn virtue, rnaketh vain
The unprevailing malice of my foe,
Whose bootless rage heaps torments for the brave,
Adds impotent eternities to pain,
Whilst keenest disappointment racks his breast
To see the smiles of peace around them play;
To frustrate, or to sanctify their doom.

Thus have I stood,—through a wild waste of years
Struggling with whirlwinds of mad agony,
Yet peaceful, and serene, and self-enshrined,
Mocking my powerless tyrant's horrible curse
With stubborn and unalterable will,
Even as a giant oak, which heaven's fierce flame
Had scathed in the wilderness, to stand.
A monument of fadeless ruin there;
Yet peacefully and movelessly it braves
The midnight conflict of the wintry storm,
    As in the sun-light's calm it spreads
    Its worn and withered arms on high
To meet the quiet of a summer's noon.

        The Fairy waved her wand;
        Ahasuerus fled
Fast as the shapes of mingled shade and mist,
That lurk in the glens of a twilight grove,
        Flee from the morning beam:
    The matter of which dreams are made

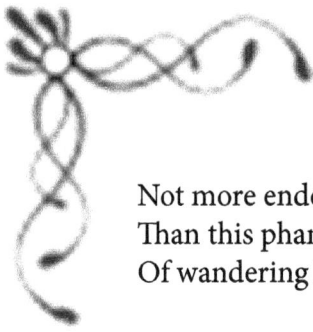

Not more endowed with actual life
Than this phantasmal portraiture
Of wandering human thought.

VIII

THE present and the past thou hast beheld:
It was a desolate sight. Now, Spirit, learn
   The secrets of the future.—Time!
Unfold the brooding pinion of thy gloom,
Render thou up thy half-devoured babes,
And from the cradles of eternity,
Where millions lie lulled to their portioned sleep
By the deep murmuring stream of passing things,
Tear thou that gloomy shroud.—Spirit, behold
     Thy glorious destiny!

     Joy to the Spirit came.
Through the wide rent in Time's eternal veil,
Hope was seen beaming through the mists of fear:
     Earth was no longer hell;
     Love, freedom, health, had given
Their ripeness to the manhood of its prime,
     And all its pulses beat
Symphonious to the planetary spheres:
     Then dulcet music swelled
Concordant with the life-strings of the soul ;
It throbbed in sweet and languid beatings there,
Catching new life from transitory death,—
Like the vague sighings of a wind at even,
That wakes the wavelets of the slumbering sea
And dies on the creation of its breath,
And sinks and rises, fails and swells by fits:
   Was the pure stream of feeling
That sprung from these sweet notes,
   And o'er the Spirit's human sympathies
With mild and gentle motion calmly flowed.

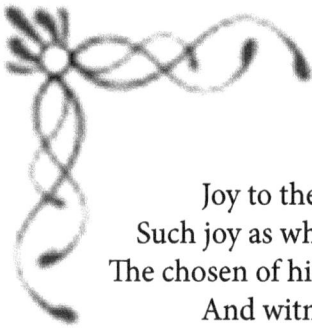

Joy to the Spirit came,—
Such joy as when a lover sees
The chosen of his soul in happiness,
And witnesses her peace
Whose woe to him were bitterer than death,
Sees her unfaded cheek
Glow mantling in first luxury of health,
Thrills with her lovely eyes,
Which like two stars amid the heaving main
Sparkle through liquid bliss.

Then in her triumph spoke the Fairy Queen:
I will not call the ghost of ages gone
To unfold the frightful secrets of its lore;
The present now is past,
And those events that desolate the earth
Have faded from the memory of Time,
Who dares not give reality to that
Whose being I annul. To me is given
The wonders of the human world to keep,
Space, matter, time, and mind. Futurity
Exposes now its treasure; let the sight
Renew and strengthen all thy failing hope.

0 human Spirit! spur thee to the goal
Where virtue fixes universal peace,
And midst the ebb and flow of human things,
Shew somewhat stable, somewhat certain still,
A lighthouse o'er the wild of dreary waves.

The habitable earth is full of bliss;
Those wastes of frozen billows that were hurled
By everlasting snow-storms round the poles,
Where matter dared not vegetate or live,
But ceaseless frost round the vast solitude

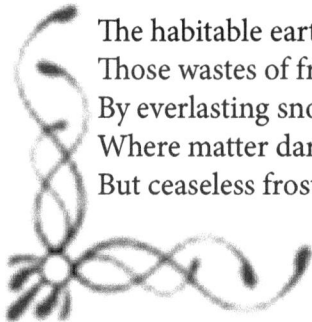

66

Bound its broad zone of stillness, are unloosed;
And fragrant zephyrs there from spicy isles
Ruffle the placid ocean-deep that rolls
Its broad, bright surges to the sloping sand,
Whose roar is wakened into echoings sweet
To murmur through the heaven-breathing groves
And melodize with man's blest nature there.

Those deserts of immeasurable sand,
Whose age-collected fervours scarce allowed
A bird to live, a blade of grass to spring,
Where the shrill chirp of the green lizard's love
Broke on the sultry silentness alone,
Now teem with countless rills and shady woods,
Corn-fields, and pastures, and white cottages;
And where the startled wilderness beheld
A savage conqueror stained in kindred blood,
A tygress sating with the flesh of lambs,
The unnatural famine of her toothless cubs,
Whilst shouts and howlings through the desert rang,
Sloping and smooth the daisy-spangled lawn,
Offering sweet incense to the sun-rise, smiles
To see a babe before his mother's door,
          Sharing his morning's meal
With the green and golden basilisk
          That comes to lick his feet.

Those trackless deeps, where many a weary sail
Has seen above the illimitable plain,
Morning on night, and night on morning rise,
Whilst still no land to greet the wanderer spread
Its shadowy mountains on the sun--bright sea,
Where the loud roarings of the tempest-waves
So long have mingled with the gusty wind
In melancholy loneliness, and swept

Those trackless deeps, where many a weary sail
Has seen above the illimitable plain,
Morning on night, and night on morning rise,
Whilst still no land to greet the wanderer spread
Its shadowy mountains on the sun--bright sea,
Where the loud roarings of the tempest-waves
So long have mingled with the gusty wind
In melancholy loneliness, and swept
The desert of those ocean solitudes,
But vocal to the sea-bird's harrowing shriek,
The bellowing monster, and the rushing storm,
Now to the sweet and many mingling sounds
Of kindliest human impulses respond.
Those lonely realms bright garden-isles begem,
With lightsome clouds and shining seas between,
And fertile vallies resonant with bliss,
Whilst green woods overcanopy the wave,
Which like a toil-worn labourer leaps to shore,
To meet the kisses of the flowrets there.

All things are recreated, and the flame
Of consentaneous love inspires all hie:
The fertile bosom of the earth gives suck
To myriads, who still grow beneath her care,
Who stands amid the ever-varying world,
The burthen or the glory of the earth;
He chief perceives the change, his being notes
The gradual renovation, and defines
Each movement of its progress on his mind.

Man, where the gloom of the long polar night
Lowers o'er the snow-clad rocks and frozen soil,
Where scarce the hardiest herb that braves the frost
Basks in the moonlight's ineffectual glow,
Shrank with the plants, and darkened with the night;

68

His chilled and narrow energies, his heart,
Insensible to courage, truth, or love,
His stunted stature and imbecile frame,
Marked him for some abortion of the earth,
Fit compeer of the bears that roamed around,
Whose habits and enjoyments were his own:
His life a feverish dream of stagnant woe,
Whose meagre wants but scantily fulfilled,
Apprised him ever of the joyless length
Which his short being's wretchedness had reached;
His death a pang, which famine, cold, and toil
Long on the mind, whilst yet the vital spark
Clung to the body stubbornly, had brought:
All was inflicted here that earth's revenge
Could wreak on the infringers of her law;
One curse alone was spared— — — — —

Nor where the tropics bound the realms of day
With a broad belt of mingling cloud and flame,
Where blue mists through the unmoving atmosphere
Scattered the seeds of pestilence, and fed
Unnatural vegetation, where the land
Teemed with all earthquake, tempest, and disease,
Was man a nobler being; slavery
Had crushed him to his country's blood-stained dust;
Or he was bartered for the fame of power,
Which all internal impulses destroying,
Makes human will an article of trade;
Or he was changed with Christians for their gold,
And dragged to distant isles, where to the sound
Of the flesh-mangling scourge, he does the work
Of all-polluting luxury and wealth,
Which doubly visits on the tyrants' heads
The long-protracted fulness of their woe;
Or he was led to legal butchery,

To turn to worms beneath that burning sun,
Where kings first leagued against the rights of men,
And priests first traded with the name of God.

Even where the milder zone afforded man
A seeming shelter, yet contagion there,
Blighting his being with unnumbered ills,
Spread like a quenchless fire ; nor truth till late
Availed to arrest its progress, or create
That peace which first in bloodless victory waved
Her snowy standard o'er this favoured clime:
There man was long the train-bearer of slaves,
The mimic of surrounding misery,
The jackal! of ambition's lion-rage,
The bloodhound of religion's hungry zeal.
Here now the human being stands adorning
This loveliest earth, with taintless body and mind;
Blest from his birth with all bland impulses,
Which gently in his noble bosom wake
All kindly passions and all pure desires.
Him, still from hope to hope the bliss pursuing,
Which from the exhaustless lore of human weal
Draws on the virtuous mind, the thoughts that rise
In time-destroying infiniteness, gift
With self-enshrined eternity, that mocks
The unprevailing hoariness of age,
And man, once fleeting o'er the transient scene
Swift as an unremembered vision, stands
immortal upon earth: no longer now
He slays the lamb that looks him in the face,
And horribly devours his mangled flesh,
Which still avenging nature's broken law,
Kindled all putrid humours in his frame,
All evil passions, and all vain belief,
Hatred, despair, and loathing in his mind,

The germs of misery, death, disease, and crime.
No longer now the winged habitants,
That in the woods their sweet lives sing away,
Flee from the form of man; but gather round,
And prune their sunny feathers on the hands
Which little children stretch in friendly sport
Towards these dreadless partners of their play.
All things are void of terror: man has lost
His terrible prerogative, and stands
An equal amidst equals: happiness
And science dawn though late upon the earth;

IX

O HAPPY Earth! reality of Heaven!
To which those restless souls that ceaselessly
Throng through the human universe, aspire;
Thou consummation of all mortal hope!
Thou glorious prize of blindly-working will!
Whose rays diffused throughout all space and time,
Verge to one point and blend for ever there:
Of purest spirits thou pure dwelling-place!
Where care and sorrow, impotence and crime,
Languor, disease, and ignorance, dare not come:
O happy Earth, reality of Heaven!

Genius has seen thee in her passionate dreams,
And dim forebodings of thy loveliness
Haunting the human heart, have there entwined
Those rooted hopes of some sweet place of bliss
Where friends and lovers meet to part no more.
Thou art the end of all desire and will,
The product of all action: and the souls
That by the paths of an aspiring change
Have reached thy haven of perpetual peace,
There rest from the eternity of toil
That framed the fabric of thy perfectness.
Yet like the bee returning to her queen,
She bound the sweetest on her sister's brow,
Who, meek and sober, kissed the sportive child,
No longer trembling at the broken rod.

Mild was the slow necessity of death:
The tranquil Spirit failed beneath its grasp,
Without a groan, almost without a fear,
Calm as a voyager to some distant land,
And full of wonder, full of hope as he.

The deadly germs of languor and disease
Died in the human frame, and purity
Blest with all gifts her earthly worshippers.
How vigorous then the athletic form of age!
How clear its open and unwrinkled brow!
Where neither avarice, cunning, pride, nor care,
Had stamped the seal of grey deformity
On all the mingling lineaments of time..
How lovely the intrepid front of youth!
Which meek-eyed courage decked with freshest grace;
Courage of soul, that dreaded not a name,
And elevated will, that journeyed on
Through life's phantasmal scene in fearlessness,
With virtue, love, and pleasure, hand in hand.

Then, that sweet bondage which is freedom's self,
And rivets with sensation's softest tie
The kindred sympathies of human souls,
Needed no fetters of tyrannic law:
Those delicate and timid impulses
In nature's primal modesty arose,
And with undoubting confidence disclosed
The growing longings of its dawning love,
Unchecked by dull and selfish chastity,
That virtue of the cheaply virtuous,
Who pride themselves in senselessness and frost.
No longer prostitution's venomed bane
Poisoned the springs of happiness and life;
Woman and man, in confidence and love,
Equal, and free, and pure, together trod
The mountain-paths of virtue, which no more
Were stained with blood from many a pilgrim's feet.

Then, where, through distant ages, long in pride
The palace of the monarch-slave had mocked

Famine's faint groan, and penury's silent tear,
A heap of crumbling ruins stood, and threw
Year after year their stones upon the field,
Wakening a lonely echo; and the leaves
Of the old thorn, that on the topmost tower
Usurped the royal ensign's grandeur, shook
In the stern storm that swayed the topmost tower
And whispered strange tales in the whirlwind's ear.

Low through the lone cathedral's roofless aisles
The melancholy winds a death-dirge sung:
It were a sight of awfulness to see
The works of faith and slavery, so vast,
So sumptuous, yet so perishing withal!
Even as the corpse that rests beneath its wall.
Now Time his dusky pennons o'er the scene
Closes in stedfast darkness, and the past
Fades from our charmed sight. My task is done:
Thy lore is learned. Earth's wonders are thine own,
With all the fear and all the hope they bring.
My spells are past: the present now recurs.
Ah me! a pathless wilderness remains
Yet unsuhdued by man's reclaiming hand.

Yet, human Spirit, bravely hold thy course,
Let virtue teach thee firmly to pursue
The gradual paths of an aspiring change:
For birth, and life, and death, and that strange state
Before the naked soul has found its home,
All tend to perfect happiness, and urge
The restless wheels of being on their way,
Whose flashing spokes, instinct with infinite life,
Bicker and burn to gain their destined goal:
For birth but wakes the spirit to the sense
Of outward shews, whose unexperienced shape

New modes of passion to its frame may lend;
Life is its state of action, and the store
•Of all events is aggregated there
That variegate the eternal universe;
Death is a gate of dreariness and gloom,
That leads to azure isles and beaming skies
And happy regions of eternal hope.
Therefore, O Spirit! fearlessly bear On :
Though storms may break the primrose on its stalk,
Though frosts may blight the freshness of its bloom,
Yet spring's awakening breath will woo the earth,
To feed with kindliest dews its favourite flower,
That blooms in mossy banks and darksome glens,
Lighting the greenwood with its sunny smile.

Fear not then, Spirit, death's disrobing hand,
So welcome when the tyrant is awake,
So welcome when the bigot's hell-torch burns;
'Tis but the voyage of a darksorne hour,
The transient gulph-dream of a startling sleep.
Death is no foe to virtue: Earth has seen
Love's brightest roses on the scaffold bloom,
Mingling with freedom's fadeless laurels there,
And presaging the truth of visioned bliss.
Are there not hopes within thee, which this scene
Of linked and gradual being has confirmed?
Whose stingings bade thy heart look further still,
When to the moonlight walk by Henry led,
Sweetly and sadly thou didst talk of death?
And wilt thou rudely tear them from thy breast,
Listening supinely to a bigot's creed,
Or tamely crouching to the tyrant's rod,
Whose iron thongs are red with human gore?
Never: but bravely bearing on, thy will,
Is destined an eternal war to wage

76

With tyranny and falsehood, and uproot
The germs of misery from the human heart.
Thine is the hand whose piety would soothe
The thorny pillow of unhappy crime,
Whose impotence an easy pardon gains,
Watching its wanderings as a friend's disease:
Thine is the brow whose mildness would defy
Its fiercest rage, and brave its sternest will,
When fenced by power and master of the world.
Thou art sincere and good; of resolute mind,
Free from heart-withering custom's cold controul,
Of passion lofty, pure and unsubduecl.
Earth's pride and meanness could not vanquish thee,
And therefore art thou worthy of the boon
Which thou hast now received: virtue shall keep
Thy footsteps in the path that thou hast trod,
And many days of beaming hope shall bless
Thy spotless life of sweet and sacred love.
Go, happy one, and give that bosom joy
   Whose sleepless spirit waits to catch
   Light, life, and rapture from thy smile.

   The Fairy waves her wand of charm.
Speechless with bliss the Spirit mounts the car,
   That rolled beside the battlement,
Bending her beamy eyes in thankfulness.
   Again the enchanted steeds were yoked,
   Again the burning wheels inflame
The steep descent of heaven's untrodden way.
   Fast and far the chariot flew:
   The vast and fiery globes that rolled
   Around the Fairy's palace-gate
Lessened by slow degrees, and soon appeared
Such tiny twinklers as the planet orbs
That there attendant on the solar power

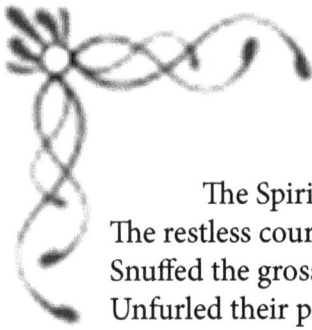

The Spirit then descended:
The restless coursers pawed the ungenial soil,
Snuffed the gross air, and then, their errand done,
Unfurled their pinions to the winds of heaven.

The Body and the Soul united then,
A gentle start convulsed Ianthe's frame:
Her veiny eyelids quietly unclosed;
Moveless awhile the dark blue orbs remained:
She looked around in wonder and beheld
Henry, who kneeled in silence by her couch,
Watching her sleep with looks of speechless love,
　　And the bright beaming stars
　　That through the casement shone.

NOTES

It will be seen by the author of QUEEN MAB, and those few gentlemen who have a copy of the former edition, that I have been studious in adhering to the original copy. The notes in French, Latin, and Greek are printed verbatim, as the classical scholar would prefer them in the language they were originally written in, and the general reader in translation.
W. CLARK.

I. PAGE 12.
The sun's unclouded orb
Rolled through the black concave.

BEYOND our atmosphere the sun would appear a rayless orb of fire in the midst of a black concave. The equal diffusion of its light on earth is owing to the refraction of the rays by the atmosphere, and their reflection from other bodies. Light consists either of vibrations propagated through a subtle medium, or of numerous minute particles repelled in all directions from the luminous body. Its velocity greatly exceeds that of any substance with which we are acquainted: observations on the eclipses of Jupiter's satellites have demonstrated that light takes up no more than 8' 7" in passing from the sun to the earth, a distance of 95,000,000 miles. Some idea may be gained of the immense distance of the fixed stars, when it is computed that many years would elapse before light could reach this earth from the nearest of them; yet in one year light travels 5,422,400,000,000 miles, which is a distance 5,707,600 times greater than that of the sun from the earth.

I. PAGE 12.
Whilst round the chariot's way
Innumerable systems rolled.

The plurality of worlds, the indefinite immensity of the universe is a most awful subject of contemplation. He who rightly feels its mystery and grandeur, is in no danger of seduction from the falsehoods of religious systems, or of deifying the principle of the universe. It is impossible to believe that the Spirit that pervades this infinite machine, is angered at the consequences of that necessity, which is a synonyme of itself. All that miserable tale of the Devil, and Eve, is irreconcileable with the knowledge of the stars. The nearest of the fixed stars is inconceivably distant from the earth, and they are probably proportionably distant from each other. By a calculation of the velocity of light, Syrius is supposed to be at least 54,224,000,000,000 miles from the earth[a]. That which

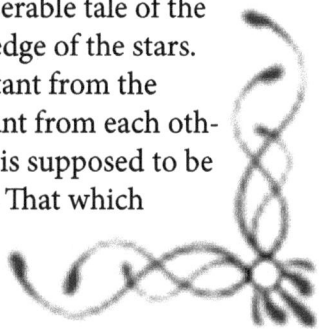

appears only like a thin and silvery cloud streaking the heaven, is in effect composed of innumerable clusters of suns, each shining with its own light, and illuminating numbers of planets that revolve around them. Millions and millions of suns are ranged around us, all attended by innumerable worlds, yet calm, regular, and harmonious, all keeping the paths of immutable necessity.
—ᴬSee Nicholson's Encyclopcedia, art. Light.

IV. PAGE 38.

These are the hired bravoes who defend
The tyrant's throne.

To employ murder as a means of justice, is an idea which a man of an enlightened mind will not dwell upon with pleasure. To march forth in rank and file,with all the pomp of streamers and trumpets, for the purpose of shooting at our fellow-men as a mark; to inflict upon them all the variety of wound and anguish; to leave them weltering in their blood; to wander over the field of desolation, and count the number of the dying and the dead,—are employments which in thesis we may maintain to be necessary, but which no good man will contemplate with gratulation and delight. A battle we suppose is won:—thus truth is established;—thus the cause of justice is confirmed! It surely requires no common sagacity to discern the connection between this immense heap of calamities, and the assertion of truth, or the maintenance of justice. Kings, and ministers of state, the real authors of the calamity, sit unmolested in their cabinet, while those against whom the fury of the s:orrn is directed, are, for the most part, persons who have been trepanned into the service, or who are dragged unwillingly from their peaceful homes into the field of battle. A soldier is a man whose business it is to kill those who never of feuded him, and who are the innocent martyrs of other men's iniquities. Whatever may become of the abstract question of the justifiableness of war, it seems impossible that the soldier should not be a depraved and unnatural being.

To these more serious and momentous considerations it may ,be proper to add a recollection of the ridiculousness of the military character. Its first constituent is obedience: a soldier is, of all descriptions of men, the most completely a machine; yet his profession inevitably teaches him something of dogmatism, swaggering, and self-consequence: he is like the puppet of a showman, who, at the very time he is made to strut and swell and display the most farcical airs, we perfectly know cannot assume the most insignificant gesture, advance either to the right or the left, but as be is moved by his exhibitor.—Godwin's Enquirer, Essay V.

I will here subjoin a little poem, so strongly expressive of my abhorrence of despotism and falsehood, that I fear lest it never again may be depictured so vividly. This opportunity is perhaps the only one that ever will occur of rescuing it from oblivion.

FALSEHOOD AND VICE.
A DIALOGUE.

Whilst monarchs laughed upon their thrones
To hear a famished nations groans,
And hugged the wealth wrung from the woe
That makes its eyes and veins o'erflow,
Those thrones, high built upon the heaps
Of bones where frenzied famine sleeps.
Where slavery wields her scourge of iron,
Red with mankind's unheeded gore,
And war's mad fiends the scene environ,
Mingling with shrieks a drunken roar,
There Vice and Falsehood took their stand,
High raised above the unhappy land.

FALSEHOOD.
Brother ! arise from the dainty fare,
Which thousands have toiled and bled to bestow;
A finer feast for thine hungry ear
Is the news that I bring of human woe.

83

VICE.

And, secret one, what hast thou done,
To compare, in thy tumid pride, with me?
I, whose career, through the blasted year,
Has been tracked by despair and agony.

FALSEHOOD.

What have I done!—I have torn the robe
From baby truth's unsheltered form,
And round the desolated globe
Borne safely the bewildering charm:
My tyrant-slaves to a dungeon-floor
Have bound the fearless innocent,
And streams of fertilizing gore
Flow from her bosom's hideous rent,
Which this unfailing dagger gave.....
I dread that blood!—no more—this day
Is ours, though her eternal ray
Must shine upon our grave.
Yet know, proud Vice, had I not given
T6 thee the robe I stole from heaven,
Thy shape of ugliness and fear
Had never gained, admission here.

VICE.

And know, that had I disdained to toil,
But sate in my loathsome cave the while,
And ne'er to these hateful sons of heaven,
GOLD, MONARCHY, and MURDER given:
Hadst thou with all thine art essayed
One of thy games then to have played,
With all thine overweening boast,
Falsehood! I tell thee thou hadst lost!—
Yet wherefore this dispute?—we tend,
Fraternal, to one common end;

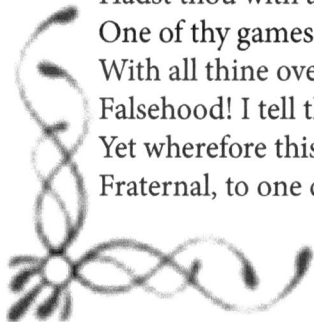

84

In this cold grave beneath my feet,
Will our hopes, our fears, and our labours meet.

FALSEHOOD.

I brought my daughter, on earth:
She smothered Reason's babes in their birth;
But dreaded their mother's eye severe,—
So the crocodile slunk off slily in fear,
And loosed her bloodhounds from the den..........
They started from dreams of slaughtered men,
And, by the light of her poison eye,
Did her work o'er the wide earth frightfully:
The dreadful stench of her torches flare,
Fed with human fat, polluted the air:
The curses, the shrieks, the ceaseless cries
Of the many-mingling miseries,
As on she trod, ascended high
And trumpeted my victory!—
Brother, tell what thou hast done.

VICE.

I have extinguished the noon-day sun,
In the carnage-smoke of battles won:
Famine, murder, hell, and power,
Were glutted in that glorious hour
Which searchless fate had stamped for me
With the seal of her security......
For the bloated wretch on yonder throne
Commanded the bloody fray to rise:
Like me he joyed at the stifled moan
Wrung from a nation's miseries;
While the snakes, whose slime even him defiled,
In ecstasies of malice smiled:
They thought 'twas theirs,—but mine the deed!
Theirs is the toil, but mine the meed—

Ten thousand victims madly bleed.
They dream that tyrants goad them there
With poisonous war to taint the air:
These tyrants, on their beds of thorn,
Swell with the thoughts of murderous fame,
And with their gains to lift my name.
Restless they plan from night to morn:
I—I do all; without my aid
Thy daughter, that relentless maid,
Could never o'er a death-bed urge
The fury of her venomed scourge.

FALSEHOOD.

Brother, well:—the world is ours;
And whether thou or I have won,
The pestilence expectant lowers
On all beneath yon blasted sun.
Our joys, our toils, our honours meet
In the milk-white and wormy winding-sheet:
A short-lived hope, unceasing care,
Some heartless scraps of godly prayer,
A moody curse, and a frenzied sleep
Ere gapes the graves unclosing deep,
A tyrant's dream, a coward's start,
The ice that clings to a priestly heart,
A judge's frown, a courtier's smile,
Make the great whole for which we toil;
And, brother, whether thou or I
Have done the work of misery,
It little boots: thy toil and pain,
Without my aid were more than vain;
And but for thee I ne'er had sate
The guardian of heaven's palace gate.

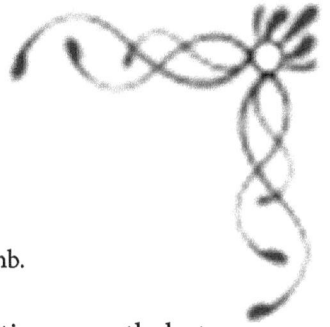

V. PAGE 42.

Thus do the generations of the earth
Go to the grave, and issue front the womb.

One generation passeth away and another generation cometh, but the earth abideth for ever. The sun also ariseth and the sun goeth down, and hasteth to his place where he arose. The wind goeth toward the south and turneth about unto the north, it whirleth about continually, and the wind returneth again, according to his circuits. All the rivers run into the sea, yet the sea is not full; unto the place whence the rivers come, thither shall they return again. Ecclesiastes, chap. i.

V. PAGE 42.

Even as the leaves
Which the keen frost-wind of the waning year
Has scattered on the forest soil.

Οἴη περ φύλλων γενεὴ, καὶ ανδρῶν.
Φύλλα τὰ μέν τ᾽ ἄνεμος χαμάδις χέει, ἄλλα δέθύλη
Τηλεθόωσα φύει, ἔαρος δἐπιγίγνεται ὥρη.
Ὥς ἀνδρῶν γενεὴ, ἡ μὲν φύει ἠδ᾽ ἀπολήγει[a].
ΙΛΙΑΔ. Ζʹ. 1. 146.
——[a]Like leaves on trees the race of man is found,
Now green in youth, now withering on the ground;
Another race the following spring supplies;
They fall successive, and successive rise:
So generations in their course decay;
So flourish these, when those are past away.
Pope's Homer.

V. PAGE 44.

The mob of peasants, nobles, priests, and kings.

Suave mari magno turbantibus æquora ventis
E terrâ magnum alterius spectare laborem;
Non quia vexari quemquam 'st jucunda voluptas,
Sed quibus ipse malis careas quia cernere suave 'st.
Suave etiam belli certamina magna tueri,
Per campos instructa, tua sine parte pericli;
Sed nil dulcius est bene quam munita tenere
Edita doctrina sapientum templa serena;
Despicere unde queas alios, passim que videre
Errare atque viam palanteis quærere vitæ;
Certare ingenio; contendere nobilitate;
Nocteis atque dies niti præstante labore
Ad summas emergere opes, rerum que potiri.
0 miseras hominum menteis! 0 pectora cæca[a]!
Luc. lib. ii.
——[a]When the wide ocean maddening whirlwinds sweep,
And heave the billows of the boiling deep,
Pleased we from land the reeling bark survey,
And rolling mountains of the watery way.
Not that we joy another's woes to see,
But to reflect that we ourselves are free.
So, the dread battle ranged in distant fields,
Ourselves secure, a secret pleasure yields.
But what more charming than to gain the height
Of true philosophy? What pure delight
From Wisdom's citadel to view below,
Deluded mortals, as they wandering go
In quest of happiness! ah, blindly weak!
For fame, for vain nobility they seek;

V. PAGE 45.
And statesmen boast
Of wealth!

There is no real wealth but the labour of man. Were the mountains of gold, and the vallies of silver, the world would not be one grain of corn the richer; no one comfort would be added to the human race. In consequence of our consideration for the precious metals, one man is enabled to heap to himself luxuries at the expence of the necessaries of his neighbour; a system admirably fitted to produce all the varieties of disease and crime, which never fail to characterise the two extremes of opulence and penury. A speculator takes pride to himself as the promoter of his country's prosperity, who employs a number of hands in the manufacture of articles avowedly destitute of use, or subservient only to the unhallowed cravings of luxury and ostentation. The nobleman, who employs the peasants of his neighbourhood in building his palaces, until "Jam pauca aratro jugera, regice moles relinquunt[a]," flatters himself that he has gained the title of a patriot by yielding to the impulses of vanity. The shew and pomp of courts adduces the same apology for its continuance; and many a fête has been given, many a woman has eclipsed her beauty by her dress, to benefit the labouring poor and to encourage trade. Who does not see that this is a remedy which aggravates, whilst it palliates the countless diseases of society? The poor are set to labour,—for what? Not the food for which they famish: not the blankets for want of which their babes are frozen by the cold of their miserable hovels: not those comfors of civilization without which civilized man is far more miserable than the meanest savage; oppressed as he is by all its insidious evils, within the daily and taunting prospect of its innumerable benefits assiduously exhibited before him:—no; for the pride of power, for the miserable isolation of pride, for the false pleasures of the hundredth part of society. No greater evidence is afforded of the wide extended and radical mistakes of civilized man than this fact: those arts which are essential to his very being are held in the greatest contempt; employments are lucrative in an inverse ratio to their usefulness[b]": the jeweller, the toyman, the actor gains fame and wealth by the exercise of his useless and ridiculous art; whilst the cultivator of the earth, be without whom society must cease to subsist, struggles through contempt and penury, and perishes by that famine which, but for his unceasing exertions,'wotild annihilate the rest of mankind.

I will not insult common sense by insisting on the doctrine of the natural equality of man. 'The question is not concerning its desirableness, but its practicability: so far as it is practicable, it is desirable. That state of human society which approaches nearer to an equal partition of its benefits and evils should, ece,teri* paribus[c], be preferred: but so long as we conceive that a wanton expenditure of human labour, not for the necessities, not even for the luxuries of the mass of society, but for the egotism and ostentation of a few of its members, is defensible on the ground of publicjustice, so long we neglect to approximate to the redemption of the human race.

Labour is required for physical, and leisure for moral improvement: from the former of these advantages the rieh, and from the latter the poor, by the inevitable condition of their respective situations, are precluded. A state which should combine the advantages of both, would be subjected to the evils of neither. He that is deficient in firm health, or vigorous intellect, is but half a man: hence it follows, that, to subject the labouring classes to unnecessary labour, is 'wantonly depriving them of any opportunities of intellectual improvement; and that the rich are heaping up for their own mischief the disease, lassitude and ennui by which their existence is rendered an intolerable burthen. English reformers exclaim against sinecures,—but the true pension-list is the rent-roll of the landed proprietors: wealth is a power usurped by the few, to compel the many to labour for their benefit. The laws which support this system derive their force from the ignorance and credulity of its victims: they are the result of a conspiracy of the few against the many, who are themselves obliged to purchase this

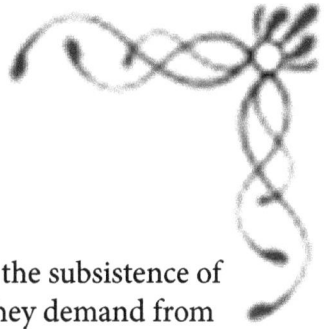

pre-eminence by the loss of all real comfort.

The commodities that substantially contribute to the subsistence of the human species form a very short catalogue: they demand from us but a slender portion of industry. If these only were produced, and sufficiently produced, the species of man would be continued. If the labour necessarily required to produce. them were equitably divided among the poor, and, still more, if it were equitably divided among all, each man's share of labour would be light, and his portion of leisure would be ample. There was a time when this leisure would have been of small comparative value: it is to be hoped that the time will come, when it will be applied to the most important purposes. Those hours which are not required for the production of the necessaries of life, may be devoted to the cultivation of the understanding, the enlarging our stock of knowledge, the refining our taste, and thus opening to us new and more exquisite sources of enjoyment.
∗∗∗

It was perhaps necessary that a period of monopoly and oppression should subsist, before a period of cultivated equality could subsist. Savages perhaps would never have been excited to the discovery of truth and the invention of art, but by the narrow motives which such a period affords. But, surely, after the savage state has ceased, and men have set out in the glorious career of discovery and invention, monopoly and oppression cannot be necessary to prevent them from returning to a state of barbarism.—Godwin's Enquirer, Essay II. See also Pol. Jus., Book VIII. chap. 11.

It is a calculation of this admirable author, that all the conveniences of civilized life might be produced, if society would divide the labour equally among its members, by each individual being employed in labour two hours during the day.

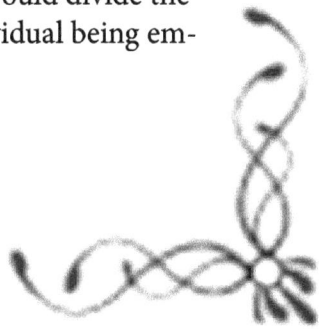

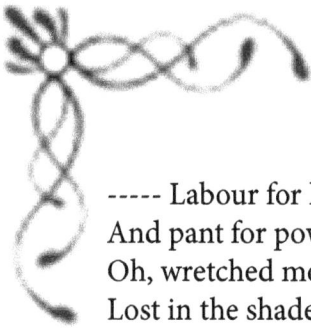

----- Labour for heapy treasures, night and day,
And pant for power and magisterial sway.
Oh, wretched mortals ! souls devoid of light,
Lost in the shades of intellectual night !
Dr. Busby's Lucretius.

[a]These piles of royal structure, will soon leave but few acres for the plough.

[b] See Rousseau, " De l'Inegalité parmi lea ommes," note'7.

[c]Making allowances on both sides.

V. PAGE 46.
Or religion
Drives his wife raving mad.

I am acquainted with a lady of considerable accomplishments, and the mother of a numerous family, whom the Christian religion has goaded to incurable insanity. A parallel case is, I believe, within the experience of every physician.

Nam jam swpe homines patriam, carosque parentes
Prodiderunt, vitare Acherusia templa petentes[a].
Lucretius.

---[a]For some, the approach of Death and Hell to stay,
Their parents, friends, and country, will betray.
Dr. Busby's Lucretius.

Not even the intercourse of the sexes is exempt from the des-
potism of positive institution. Law pretends even to govern the
indisciplinable wanderings of passion, to put fetters on the clearest
deductions of reason, and, by appeals to the will, to subdue the
involuntary affections of our nature. Love is inevitably consequent
upon the perception of loveliness. Love withers under constraint:
its very essence is liberty: it is compatible neither with obedience,
jealousy, nor fear: it is there most pure, perfect, and unlimited,
where its votaries live in confidence, equality, and onreserve.
How long then ought the sexual connection to last? what law
ought to specify the extent of the grievances which should limit its
duration? A husband and wife ought to continue so long united as
they love each other: any law which should bind them to cohabi-
tation for one moment after the decay of their affection, would be
a most intolerable tyranny, and the most unworthy of toleration.
How odious an usurpation of the right of private judgment should
that law be considered, which should make the ties of friendship
indissoluble, in spite of the caprices, the inconstancy, the fallibil-
ity, and capacity for improvement of the human mind. And by so
much would the fetters of love be heavier and more unendurable
than those of friendship, as love is more vehement and capricious,
more dependent on those delicate peculiarities of imagination,
and less capable of reduction to the ostensible merits of the object.
The state of society in which we exist is a mixture of feudal sav-
ageness and imperfect civilization. The narrow and unenlightened
morality of the Christian religion is an aggravation of these evils. It
is not even until lately that mankind have admitted that happiness
is the sole end of the science of ethics, as of all other sciences; and
that the fanatical idea of mortifying the flesh for the love of God
has been discarded. I have heard, indeed, an ignorant collegian ad-
duce, in favour of Christianity, its hostility to every worldly feelin-
g[a]! But if happiness be the object of morality, of all human unions
and disunions if the worthiness of every action is to be estimated

by the quantity of pleasurable sensation it is calculated to produce, then the connection of the sexes is so long sacred as it contributes to the comfort of the parties, and is naturally dissolved when its evils are greater than its benefits. There is nothing immoral in this separation. Constancy has nothing virtuous in itself, independently of the pleasure it confers, and partakes of the temporizing spirit of vice in proportion as it endures tamely moral defects of magnitude in the object of its indiscreet choice. Love is free: to promise for ever to love the same woman, is not less absurd than to promise to believe the same creed: such a vow, in both cases, excludes us from all enquiry. The language of the votarist is this: The woman I now love may be infinitely inferior to many others; the creed I now profess may be a mass of errors and absurdities; but I exclude myself from all future information as to the amiability of the one, and the truth of the other, resolving blindly, and in spite of conviction, to adhere to them.--Is this the language of delicacy and reason? Is the love of such a frigid heart of more worth than its belief? The present system of constraint does no more, in the majority of instances, than make hypocrites or open enemies. Persons of delicacy and virtue, unhappily united to one whom they find it impossible to love, spend the loveliest season of their life in unproductive efforts to appear otherwise than they are, for the sake of the feelings of their partner or the welfare of their mutual offspring: those of less generosity and refinement openly avow their disappointment, and linger out the remnant of that union, which only death can dissolve, in a state of incurable bickering and hostility. The early education of their children takes its colour from the squabbles of the parents; they are nursed in a systematic school of ill-humour, violence, and falsehood. Had they been suffered to part at the moment when indifference rendered their union irksome, they would have been spared many years of misery: they would have connected themselves more suitably, and would have found that happiness in the society of more congenial partners which is for ever denied them by the despotism of marriage. They would have been separately useful and happy members of society, who, whilst united, were miserable, and rendered misanthropical by misery. The conviction that wedlock is indissoluble holds out the strongest of all temptations to the perverse: they indulge without restraint in acrimony, and all the little tyrannies of domestic life, when they know that their victim is without appeal. If this connection were put on a rational basis, each would be assured that habitual ill temper would terminate in separation, and would check this vicious and dangerous propensity. Prostitution is the legitimate offspring of marriage and its accompanying errors. Women, for no other crime than having followed the dictates of a natural appetite, are driven with fury from the comforts and sympathies of society. It is less venial than murder; and the punishment which is inflicted on her who destroys her child to escape reproach, is lighter than the life of agony and disease to which the prostitute is irrecoverably doomed. Has a woman obeyed the impulse of unerring nature;—society declares war against her, pityless and eternal war: she must be the tame slave, she must make no reprisals; theirs is the right of persecution, hers the duty of endurance. She lives a life of infamy: the loud and bitter laugh of scorn scares her from all return. She dies of long and lingering disease: yet she is in fault, she is.the criminal, she the froward and untameable child,—and society, forsooth, the pure and virtuous matron, who casts her as an abortion from her undefiled bosom! Society avenges herself on the criminals of her own creation; she is employed in anathematizing the vice to-day, which yesterday she was the most zealous to teach. Thus is formed one-tenth of the population of London: meanwhile the evil is twofold. Young men, excluded by the fanatical idea of chastity from the society of modest and accomplished women, associate with these vicious and miserable beings, destroying thereby all those exquisite and delicate sensibilities whose existence cold-hearted worldlings have denied; annihilating all genuine passion, and debasing that to a selfish feeling which is the excess of generosity and devotedness. Their body and mind alike crumble into a hideous wreck of humanity; idiotcy and disease become perpetuated in their miserable offspring, and distant generations suffer for the

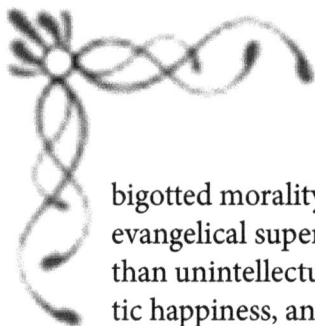

bigotted morality of their forefathers. Chastity is a monkish and evangelical superstition, a greater foe to natural temperance even than unintellectual sensuality; it strikes at the root of all domestic happiness, and consigns more than half of the human race to misery, that some few may monopolize according to law. A system could not well have been devised more studiously hostile to human happiness than marriage. I conceive that, from the abolition of marriage, the fit and natural arrangement of sexual connection would result. I by no means assert that the intercourse would be promiscuous: on the contrary; it appears, from the relation of parent to child, that this union is generally of long duration, and marked above all others with generosity and self-devotion. But this is a subject which it is perhaps premature to discuss. That which will result from the abolition of marriage, will be natural and right, because choice and change will be exempted from restraint. How would morality, dressed up in stiff stays and finery, start from her own disgusting image, should she look in the mirror of nature!

---[a] The first Christian emperor made a law by which seduction was punished with death; if the female pleaded her own consent, she also was punished with death; if the parents endeavoured to screen the criminals, they were banished, and their estates wete confiscated ; the slaves who might be accessary were burned alive, or forced to swallow melted lead. The very offspring of an illegal love were involved in the consequences of the sentence.—Gibbon's Decline and Fall, &c. vol. ii. page 210. See also, for the hatred of the primitive Christians to love, and even marriage, page 269.

VI. PAGE 53.
To the red and baleful sun
That faintly twinkles there.

The north polar star, to which the axis of the earth, in its present state of obliquity, points. It is exceedingly probable, from many considerations, that this obliquity will gradually diminish, until the equator coincides with the ecliptic: the nights and days will then become equal on the earth throughout the year, and probably the seasons also. There is no great extravagance in presuming that the progress of the perpendicularity of the poles may be as rapid as the progress of intellect; or that there should be a perfect identity between the moral and physical improvement of the human species. It is certain that wisdom is not compatible with disease, and that, in the present state of the climates of the earth, health, in the true and comprehensive sense of the word, is out of the reach of civilized man. Astronomy teaches us that the earth is now in its progress, and that the poles are every year becoming more and more perpendicular to the ecliptic. The strong evidence afforded by the history of mythology, and geological researches, that some event of this nature has taken place already, affords a strong presumption that this progress is not merely an oscillation, as has been surmised by some late astronomers[a]. Bones of animals peculiar to the torrid zone have been found in the north of Siberia, and on the banks of the river Ohio. Plants have been found in the fossil state in the interior of Germany, which demand the present climate of Hindostan for their production[b]. The researches of M. Bailly[c] establish the existence of a people who inhabit a tract of land in Tartary, 49° north latitude, of greater antiquity than either the Indians, the Chinese, or the Chaldeans, from whom these nations derived their sciences and theology. We find, from the testimony of ancient writers, that Britain, Germany, and France, were much colder than at present, and that their great rivers were annually frozen over. Astronomy teaches us also, that since this period the obliquity of the earth's position has been considerably diminished.

---[a] Laplace, Systeme du Monde.

[b] Cabanis, Rapports du Physique et du Moral de l'Homme, vol. ii. p.406.

[c] Lettres sur les Sciences, a Voltaire. Bailly

VI. PAGE 57.

No atom of this turbulence fulfils
A vague and unnecessitated task,
Or acts but as it must and ought to act.

Deux exemples servirent à nous rendre plus sensible le principe qui vient d'être pose; nous emprunterons l'une du physique et l'autre du moral. Dans tin tourbillon de poussiere qu'eleve un vent impetueux, quelque confus qu'il paroisse a nos yeux; dans la plus affreuse tempete excite par des vents opposes qui soulevent les fiots, il n'y a pas une seule molecule de poussiere on d'eau qui soit place au hazard, qui n'ait sa cause suffisante pour occuper le lieu of eile se trouve, et qui n'agisse rigoureussement de la maniere dont ehe doit agir. Une géomètre qui connoitroit exactement les différentes forces qui agissent dans ces deux cas, et les propriétés des molecules qui sont mues, demontreroit que d'après des causes donnes, chaque molecule agit précisément comme elle doit agir, et ne pent agir autrement qu'elle ne fait. Dans les convulsions terribles qui agitent quelquefois les sociétés politiques, et qui produisent souvent le renversement d'un empire, il n'y a pas tine seule action, une seule parole, une seule pensée, une seule volonté, une seule passion dans les agens qui concourent à la revolution comme destructeurs ou comme victimes, qui ne soit necessaire, qui n'agisse comme eile doit agir, qui n'opère infalliblement les effets qu'elle doit opérer, suivant la place qu'occupent ces agens dans ce tourbillon moral. Cela paroitroit evident pour une intelligence qui sera en état de saisir et d'apprécier toutes les actions et re-actions des esprits et des corps de ceux qui contribuent à cette revolution[a]. Systeme de la Nature, vol. i. p. 44.

[a] Two instances will serve to render more sensible to us the principle here laid down; we will borrow one from natural the other from moral philosophy. In a whirlwind of dust raised by an impetuous wind, however confused it may appear to our eyes ; in the most dreadful tempest excited by opposing winds, which convulse the waves, there is not a single particle of dust or of water that is placed by chance that has not its sufficient cause for occupying the situation in which it is, and which does not rigororously act in the mode it should act. A geometrician who knew equally the different powers which operate in both cases, and the properties of the particles which are propelled, would shew that according to the given causes, each particle acts precisely as it should act, and cannot act otherwise than it does. In those terrible convulsions which sometimes agitate political societies, and which frequently bring on the overthrow of an empire, there is not a single action, a single word, a single thought, a single volition, a single passion in the agents, which concur in the revolution as destroyers, or as victims, which is not necessary, which does not act as it should act, which does not infallibly produce the effects which it should produce, according to the place occupied by these agents in the moral whirlwind. This would appear evident to an intelligence which would be in a state to seize and appreciate all the actions and re-actions of the minds and bodies of those who contribute to this revolution. System of Nature, vol i.

VI. PAGE 58.
Necessity! thou mother of the world !

He who asserts the doctrine of Necessity, means that, contemplating the events which compose the moral and 'material universe, he beholds only an immense and uninterrupted chain of causes and effects, no one of which could occupy any other place than it does occupy, or act in any other place than it does act. The idea of necessity is obtained by our experience of the connection between objects, the uniformity of the operations of nature, the constant conjunction of similar events, and the consequent inference of one from the other. Mankind are therefore agreed in the admission of necessity, if they admit that these two circumstances take place in voluntary action. Motive is, to voluntary action in the human mind, what cause is to effect in the material universe. The word liberty, as applied to mind, is analogous to the word chance, as applied to matter: they spring from an ignorance of the certainty of the conjunction of antecedents and consequents. Every human being is irresistibly impelled to act precisely as he does act: in the eternity which preceded his birth, a chain of causes was generated, which, operating under the name of motives, make it impossible that any thought of his mind, or any action of his life, should be otherwise than it is. Were the doctrine of Necessity false, the human mind would no longer be a legitimate object of science; from like causes it would be in vain that we should expect like effects; the strongest motive would no longer be paramount over the conduct; all knowledge would be vague and undeterminate ; we could not predict with any certainty, that we might not meet as an enemy to-morrow, him with whom we have parted in friendship to-night; the most probable inducements and the clearest reasonings would lose the invariable influence they possess. The contrary of this is demonstrably the t'act. Similar circumstances produce the same unvariable effects. The precise character and motives of any man on any occasion being given, the moral philosopher could predict his actions with as much certainty as the natural philosopher could predict the effects of the mixture of any particular .chemical substances. Why is the aged husbandman more experienced than the young beginner? Because there is an uniform, undeniable necessity in the operations of the material universe. Why is the old statesman more skilful than the raw politician? Because, relying on the necessary conjunction of motive and action, he proceeds to produce moral effects, by the application of those moral bcauses which experience has .shewn to be effectual. Some actions may be found to which we can attach no motives, but these are the effects of causes with which we are unacquainted. Hence the relation which motive bears to voluntary action is that of cause to effect;

nor, placed in this point of view, is it, or ever has it been the subject of popular or philosophical dispute. None but the few fanatics who are engaged in the Herculean task of reconciling the justice of their God with the misery of man, will longer outrage common sense by the supposition of an event without a cause, a voluntary action without a motive. Uistory, politics, morals, criticism, all grounds of reasoning, all principles of science, alike assume the truth of the doctrine of Necessity. No farmer carrying his corn to market doubts the sale of it at the market price. The master of a manu-factory no more doubts that he can purchase the human labour necessary for his purposes, than that his machinery will act as they havebeen accustomed to act.. But, whilst none have scrupled to admit necessity as influencing matter, many have disputed its dominion over mind. Independently of its militating with the received ideas of the justice of God, it is by no means obvious to a superficial enquiry. When the mind observes its own operations, it feels no connection of motive and action: but as we know "nothing more of causation than the constant conjunction of objects and the consequent inference of one from the other, as we find that these two circumstances are universally allowed to have place in volun-tary action, we may be easily led to own that they are subjected to the necessity common to all causes." The actions of the will have a regular conjunction with circumstances and characters; motive is, to voluntary action, what cause is to effect. But the only idea we can form of causation is a constant conjunction of similar objects, and the consequent inference of one from the other: wherever this is the case necessity is clearly established. The idea of liberty, applied metaphorically to the will, has sprung from a misconcep-tion of the meaning of the word power. What is power?—id quod potest[a], that which can produce any given effect. To deny power, is to say that nothing can or has the power to be or act. In the only true sense of the word power, it applies with equal force to the loadstone as to the human will. Do you think these motives, which I shall present, are powerful enough to rouse him? is a question just as common as, Do you think this lever has the power of raising this weight? The advocates of free-will assert that the will has the power of refusing to be determined by the strongest motive: but the strongest motive is that which, overcoming all others, ultimately prevails; this assertion therefore amounts to a denial of the will being ultimately determined by that motive which does determine it, which is absurd. But it is equally certain that a man cannot resist the strongest motive, as that he cannot overcome a physical impossibility. The doctrine of Necessity tends to introduce a great change into the established notions of morality, and utterly to destroy religion. Reward and punishment must be considered, by the Necessarian, merely as motives which he would employ in order to procure the adoption or abandonment of any given line of conduct. Desert, in the present sense of the word, would no longer have any meaning; and he, who should inflict pain upon another for no better reason than that he deserved it, would only gratify his revenge under pretence of satisfying justice. It is not enough, says the advocate of free-will, that a criminal should be prevented from a repetition of his crime: he should feel pain, and his torments, when justly inflicted, ought precisely to be proportioned to his fault. But utility is morality; that which is incapable of producing happiness is useless; and though the crime of Damiens must be condemned, yet the frightful torments which revenge, under the name of justice, inflicted on this unhappy man, cannot be supposed to have augmented, even at the long run, the stock of pleasurable sensation in the world. At the same time the doctrine of Necessity does not in the least diminish our disapprobation of vice. The conviction which all feel, that a viper is a poisonous animal, and that a tyger is constrained, by the inevitable condition of his existence, to devour men, does not induce us to avoid them less sedulously, or, even more, to hesitate in destroying them: but he would surely be of a hard heart, who, meeting with a serpent on a desart island, or in a situation where it was incapable of injury, should wantonly deprive it of existence. A Necessarian is inconsequent to his own principles, if he indulges in hatred or contempt; the compassion which he feels for the criminal is unmixed with a desire of injuring him: he looks with an elevated and dreadless composure upon the links of the universal chain as they pass before his eyes; whilst cowardice, curiosity and inconsistency only assail him in proportion to the feebleness and indistinctness with which he has perceived and rejected the delusions of free-will. Religion is the perception of the relation in which we stand to the principle of the universe. But if the principle of the universe be not an organic being, the model and prototype of man, the relation between it and human beings is absolutely none. Without some insight into its will respecting our actions, religion is nugatory and vain. But will is only a mode of animal mind ; moral qualities also are such as only a human being can possess; to attribute them to the principle of the universe, is to annex to it properties incompatible with any possible definition of its nature. It is probable that the word God was originally only an expression denoting the unknown cause of the known events which men perceived in the universe. By the vulgar mistake of a metaphor for a real being, of a word for a thing, it became a man, endowed with human qualities and governing the universe as an earthly monarch governs his kingdom. Their addresses to this imaginary being, indeed, are much in the same style as those of subjects to a king. They acknowledge his benevolence, deprecate his anger, and supplicate his favour. But the doctrine of Necessity teaches us, that in no case could any event have happened otherwise than it did happen, and that, if God is the author of good, he is also the author of evil; that, if he is entitled to our gratitude for the one, he is entitled to our hatred for the other; that, admitting the existence of this hypothetic being, he is also subjected to the dominion of an immutable necessity. It is plain that the same arguments which prove that God is the author of food, light, and life, prove him also to be the author of poison, darkness, and death. The wide-wasting earthquake, the storm, the battle, and the tyranny, are attributable to this hypothetic being in the same degree as the fairest forms of nature, sunshine, liberty, and peace. But we are taught, by the doctrine of Necessity, that there is neither good nor evil in the universe,otherwise than

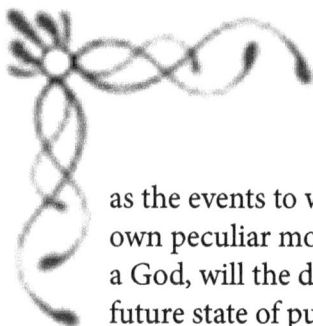

as the events to which we apply these epithets have relation to our own peculiar mode of being. Still less than with the hypothesis of a God, will the doctrine of Necessity accord with the belief of a future state of punishment. God made man such as he is: for to say that God was the author of all good, and man the author of all evil, is to say that one man made a straight line and a crooked one, and another man made the incongruity.

A Mahometan story, much to the present purpose, is recorded, wherein Adam and Moses are introduced disputing before God in the following manner. Thou, says Moses, art Adam, whom God created, and animated with the breath of life, and caused to be worshipped by the angels, and placed in Paradise, from whence mankind have been expelled for thy fault. Whereto Adam answered, Thou art Moses, whom God chose for his apostle, and entrusted with his word, by giving thee the tables of the law, and whom he vouchsafed to admit to discourse with himself. How many years dost thou find the law was written before I was created? Says Moses, Forty. And dost thou not find, replied Adam, these words therein, And Adam rebelled against his Lord and transgressed? Which Moses confessing, Post thou therefore blame me, continued he, for doing that which God wrote of me that I should do, forty years before I was created, nay, for what was decreed concerning me fifty thousand years before the creation of heaven and earth? -Sale's Prelini. Disc. to the Koran, p. 164.

--[a] That which can do any thing.

VII. PAGE 61.
There is no God!

This negation must be understood solely to affect a creative Deity.
The hypothesis of a pervading Spirit coeternal with the universe,
remains unshaken. A close examination of the validity of the
proofs adduced to support any proposition, is the only secure way
of attaining truth, on the advantages of which it is tinnecessary to
descant: our knowledge of the existence of a Deity is a subject of
such importance, that it cannot be too minutely investigated; in
consequence of this conviction we proceed briefly and impartially
to examine the proofs which have been adduced. It is necessary
first to consider the nature of belief. When a proposition is offered
to the mind, it perceives the agreement or disagreement of the
ideas of which it is composed. A perception of their agreement
is termed belief Many obstacles frequently prevent this perception
from being immediate; these the mind attempts to remove, in
order that the perception may be distinct. The mind is active in the
investigation, in order to perfect the state of perception of the re-
lation which the component ideas of the proposition bear to each,
which is passive: the investigation being confused with the percep-
tion, has induced many falsely to imagine that the mind is active
in belief,—that belief is an act of volition,—in consequence of
which it may be regulated by the mind. Pursuing, continuing this
mistake, they have attached a degree of criminality to disbelief; of
which, in its nature, it is incapable: it is equally incapable of merit.
Belief, then, is a passion, the strength of which, like every other
passion, is in precise proportion to the degreesof excitement. The
degrees of excitement are three. The senses are the sources of all
knowledge to the mind; consequently their evidence claims the
strongest assent. The decision of the mind, founded upon our own
experience, derived from these sources, claims the next degree.
The experience of others, which addresses itself to the former one,
occupies the lowest degree. (A graduated scale, on which should be
marked the capabilities of propositions to approach to the test of

the senses, would be a just barometer of the belief which ought to be attached to them.) Consequently no testimony can be admitted which is contrary to reason; reason is founded on the evidence of our senses. Every proof may be referred to one of these three divisions: it is to be considered what arguments we receive from each of them, which should convince us of the existence of a Deity. 1st. The evidence of the senses. If the Deity should appear to us, if he should convince our senses, of his existence, this revelation would necessarily command belief. Those to whom the Deity has thus appeared have the strongest possible conviction of his existence. But the God of Theologians is incapable of local visibility. 9d. Reason. It is urged that man knows that whatever is, must either have had a beginning, or have existed from all eternity: be also knows, that whatever is not eternal must have had a cause. When this reasoning is applied to the universe, it is necessary to prove that it Was created: until that is clearly demonstrated, we may reasonably suppose that it has endured from all eternity. We must prove design before we can infer a designer. The only idea which we can form of causation is derivable from the constant conjunction of objects, and the consequent inference of one from the other. In a case where two propositions are diametrically opposite, the mind believes that which is least incomprehensible;—it is easier to suppose that the universe has existed from all eternity, than to conceive a being beyond its limits capable of creating it: if the mind sinks beneath the weight of one, is it an alleviation to increase the intolerability of the burthen? The other argument, which is founded on a man's knowledge of his own existence, stands thus. A man knows not only that he now is, but that once he was not; consequently there must have been a cause. But our idea of causation is alone derivable from the constant conjunction of objects and the consequentl nference of one from the other; and, reasoning experimentally, we can only infer from effects, causes exactly adequate to those effects. But there certainly is a generative power which is effected by certain instruments we cannot prove that it is inherent in these instruments; nor is the contrary hypothesis capable of demonstration: we admit that the generative power is incomprehensible; but to suppose that the same effect is produced by an eternal, omniscient, omnipotent being, leaves the cause in the same obscurity, but renders it more incomprehensible. 3d. Testimony. It is required that testimony should not be contrary to reason. The testimony that the Deity convinces the senses of men of his existence, can only be admitted by us, if our mind considers it less probable that these men should have been deceived, than that the Deity should have appeared to them. Our reason can never admit the testimony of men, who not only declare that they were eye-witnesses of miracles, but that the Deity was irrational; for he commanded that he should be believed, he proposed the highest rewards for faith, eternal punishments for disbelief. We can only command voluntary actions; belief is not an act of volition; the mind is even passive, or involuntarily active: from this it is evident that we have no sufficient testimony, or rather that testimony is insufficient to prove the being of a God. It has been before shewn that it cannot be deduced from reason. They alone, then, who have been convinced by the evidence of the senses, can believe it.. Hence it is evident that, having no proofs from either of the three sources of conviction, the mind cannot believe the existence of a creative God: it is also evident, that, as belief is a passion of the mind, no degree of criminality is attachable to disbelief; and that they only are reprehensible who neglect to remove the false medium through which their mind views any subject of discussion. Every reflecting mind must acknowledge that there is no proof of the existence of a Deity. God is an hypothesis, and, as such, stands in need of proof: the onus probandi[a] rests on the theist. Sir Isaac Newton says: Hypotheses non lingo, quicquid enim ex phoenomenis non deducitur, hypothesis vocanda est, et hypothesis vet metaphysiece, vet physicce, vet qUalitalum occultarum, seu mechaniece, in philosophid locum non habent[b]. To all proofs of the existence of a creative God apply this valuable rule. 'We see a variety of bodies possessing a variety of powers: we merely know their effects; we are in a state of ignorance with respect to their

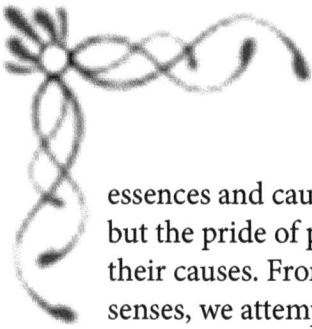

essences and causes. These Newton calls the phenomena of things; but the pride of philosophy is unwilling to admit its ignorance of their causes. From the phenomena, which are the objects of our senses, we attempt to infer a cause, which we call God, and gratuitously endow it with all negative and contradictory qualities. From this hypothesis we invent this general name, to conceal our ignorance of causes and essences. The being called God by no means answers with the conditions prescribed by Newton; it bears every mark of a veil woven by philosophical conceit, to hide the ignorance of philosophers even from themselves. They borrow the threads of its texture from the anthropomorphism of the vulgar. Words have been used by sophists for the same purposes, from the occult qualities of the peripatetics to the effluvium of Boyle and the crinities or nebulce of Herschel. God is represented as infinite, eternal, incomprehensible; he is contained under every prwdicate in non that the logic of ignorance could fabricate. Even his worshippers allow that it is impossible to form any idea of him: they exclaim with the French poet,

Pour dire ce qu'il est, it faut Ore lui-méne.[c]

Lord Bacon says, that " Atheism leaves a man to sense, to philosophy, to natural piety, to laws, to reputation: all which may be guides to an outward moral virtue, though religion were not ; but superstition dismounts all these, and erecteth an absolute monarchy in the minds of men: therefore atheism did never perturb states ; for it makes men wary of themselves, as looking no farther, and we see the times inclined to atheism (as the time of Augustus Czesar) were civil times: but superstition bath been the confusion of many states, and bringeth in a new primum mobile, that ravisheth all the spheres of government. Bacon's Moral Essay on Superstition.

La premiere theologie de l'homme lui fit d'abord craindre et adorer les élémens même, des objets matériels et grossiers; il rendit ensuite ses hommages à des agens présidens aux élémens, à des génies inférieurs, à des hèros, ou á des hommes douès de grands qualitès. A force de réfléchir il crut simplifier les choses en

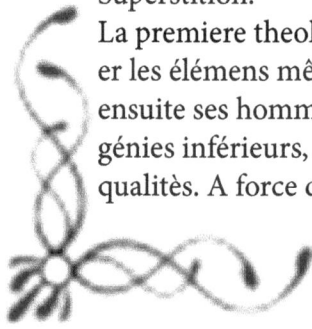

soumettant la nature entière à un seul agent, àun esprit, à une âme universelle, qui mettoit cette nature et ses parties en mouvement. En remontant des causes en causes, les mortels ont fini par ne rien voir; et c'est dans cette obscurité qu'ils ont placé leur Dieu; c'est dans cette abîme ténébreux que leur imagination inquiète travaille toujours à se fabriquer des chimères, que les afftgeront jusqu'à ce que la connoissance de la nature less détrompe des phantömes qu'ils ont toujours si vainement adorés. Si nous voulons nous rendre compte de nos idées stir la Divinité, nous serons obligés de convenir que, par le mot Dieu, les hommes n'ont jamais pu designer que la cause la plus cachée, la plus éloignée, la plus inconnue des effets qu'ils voyoient: ils ne font usage de cc mot, que lorsque le jeu des causes naturelles et connues cesse d'être visible pour eux; dès qu'ils perdent le fit de ces causes, ou dès que leur esprit ne peut plus en suivre la chaine, us tranchent leur dificulté, et terminent leur recherches en apellent Dieu la dernière des causes, c'est-à-dire celle qui est au-delà de toutes les causes qu'ils connoissent; ainsi us ne font qu'assigner tine dénomination vague à une cause ignorée, à laquelle leur paresse ou les bornes de leurs connoissances les orcent de s'arrêter. Toutes les fois qu'on nous dit que Dieu est l'auteur de quelque phénomène, cela signifie qu'on ignore comment un tel phénomène a pu s'opèrer par le sècours des forces ou des causes que nous connoissons dans la nature. C'est. ainsi que le commun des hommes, dont l'ignorance est la partage, attribue à la Divinité, non seulement les effets inusités que les frappent, mais encore les événemens les plus simples, clout les causes sont les plus faciles à connoitre pour quiconque a pu les méditer. En un mot, l'hornme a toujours respecté les causes inconnues des effets stirprenans, que son ignorance l'empêchoit de démêler. Ce fut stir les débris de la nature que les hommes é1evèrent le colosse imaginaire de la Divinité. Si l'ignoranee de la nature donna la naissance aux dieux, la connoissance de la nature est faite pour les detruire. A mésure que l'hornme s'instruit, ses forces et ses ressourees augmentent avec ses lumières; les sciences, les arts conservateurs, l'industrie, lui fournissent des seeours; l'expérience le rassûre, ou lui procure des

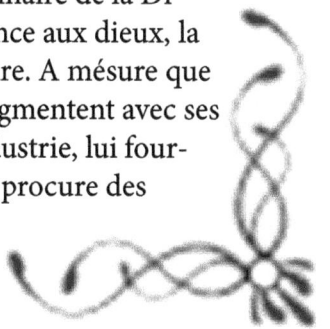

moyens de résister aux efforts de bien des causes qui cessent de l'alarmer dès qu'il les a connues. En un mot, ses terreurs se dissipent darts la meme proportion que son esprit s'éclaire. L'homrne instruit cesse d'être superstitieux. Ce n'est jamais que stir parole clue des pen pies entiers adorent le Dieu de leurs pères et de leurs prêtres: l'autorite, la confiance, la soumission, et l'habitude, leur tiennent, lieu de conviction et de preuves; is se prosternent et prient, parce que leurs pères leur ont appris à se prosterner et prier: mais pourquoi ceux-ci se son t-ils mis a genoux? C'est que dans les temps eloignes leurs législateurs et leurs guides leur en out fait un devoir. "Adorez et croyez," out-us dit, "des dieuxque vous ne pouvez comprendre; rapportez-vous en à notre sagesse profonde; nous en savons plus que vous stir la Divinité." "Mais pourquoi m'en rapporterois-je à vous?" "C'est que Dieu le veut ainsi, c'est que Dieu vous punira si vous osez résister." "Mais ce Dieu n'estil done pas la chose en question?" Cependant les hommes se sont toujours payés de ce cercle vicieux; la paresse de leur esprit leur fit trouver plus court de s'en rapporter au jugement des autres. Toutes les notions religieuses sont fondées uniquement sur l'autorité; toutes les religions du monde defendent l'examen et ne veulent pas que l'on raisonne; c'est l'autorité que veut qu'on cart en Dieu; ce Dieu n'est lui-mêne fondé que sur l'autorité de quelques hommes qui prétendent le connoitre, et venir de sa part pour l'annoncer a la terre. Uri Dieu fait par les homilies, a sans doute besoin des hommes pour se faire connoître aux hommes. Ne seroit-ce done que pour des prêtres des inspires, des nietaphysiciens que seroit reservée la conviction de l'existence d'un Dieu, que l'on dit neanmoins si necessaire a tout le genre-laurnain? Mais trouvonsnous de l'hartnonie entre les opinions théologiques des differens inspirés, ou des penseurs répandus sur la terre? Ceux mêne que font profession d'adorer le m'eme Dieu, soot-us d'accord sur son compte? Sont-ils contents des preuves que leurs collègues apportent de son existence? Souscrivent-ils unanimement aux idées qu'ils presentent sur sa nature, sur sa conduite, sur la favn d'entendre ses prétendus oracles? Est-il une contree sur la terre, où la science de Dieu se

soit réellernent perfectionné? A-t-elle pris quelque part la consis-
tence et l'uniformité que nous voyons prendre aux connoissauces
humaines, aux arts les plus futiles, aus métiers les plus meprisés?
des mots d'esprits, d'iimmatérialité, de création, de prédstination,
de grace; cette foule de distinctions subtiles dont la théologie s'est
partout remplie dans quelques pays, ces inventions si ingénieuses,
imaginées par des penseurs que se sont succédés depuis tant de
sicèles, n'ont fait, helas! qu'embrouilles les choses, et jamais le
science le plus necessaire aux hommes n'a jusqu'ici pu acquérir
la moindre fixité.Depuis des milliers d'années, ces reveurs oisifs
se sont perpétuellement relayés pour mediter la Divinité, pour
deviner ses voies cachées, pour inventer des hypotheses propres à
développer cette enigme importante. Leur peu dé succés n'a point
découragé la vanité théologique; toujours on a paelé de Dieu: on
s'est égorgé pour lui, et cet être sublime demeure toujours le plus
ignoré et le plus discuté. Les hommes auroient été trop heureux,
si, se bornant aux objets visibles qui les intéressent, us eussent
employé à perfectionner leurs sciences réelles, leurs loix, leur
morale, leur éducation, la moitié des efforts qu'ils ont mis dans
leurs recherches sur la Divinité. Ils auroient été bien plus sages
encore, et plus fortunés s'ils eussent pu consentir à laisser leurs
guides désœuvrés se quereller entre eux, et sonder des profondeurs
capables de les étourdir, sans se mêler de leurs disputes insensées.
Mais il est de l'essence de l'ignorance d'attacher de l'importance à
ce qu'elle ne comprend pas. La vanité humaine fait que l'esprit se
roidit contre les difficultés. Plus un objet se dérobe à nos yeux, plus
nous faisons d'efforts pour le saisir, parce que dès-lors il aiguillone
notre orgueil, il excite notre curiosité, il nous paroit interessant. En
combattant pour son Dieu, chacun ne combattit en effet qne pour
les intérêts de sa propre vanité, qui de tontes les passions produits
par la mal organization de la société, est la plus prompte à s'allar-
rner, et la plus propre à produire des tres grands folios. Si écartant
pour nn moment les idées facheuses que la théologie nous donne
d'un Dieu capricieux, dont les décrets parteaux et despotiques
décident du sort des humains, nous ne voulons fixer nos yeux que

sur la bonté prétendue, que tons les hommes, méme en tremblant devant ce Dieu, s'accordant à lui donner; si nous lui supposons le projet qu'on lui prête, de n'avoir travaillé que pour sa propre gloire, d'exiger les hommages des êtres intelligens; de ne chercher dans ses œuvres que le bien-être du genre humain; comment concilier ses vues et ses dispositions avec l'ignorance vraiment invincible dans laquelle ce Dien, Si glorieux et si bon, laisse la plupart des hommes sur son compte? Si Dieu veut être connu, cheri, remercié, que Ile se montre-t-il sous des traits favorables a tous ces etres intelligens dont il veut être aimê et adoré? Pourquoi ne point se manifester à toute la terre d'une façon non équiveque, bien plus capable de nous convaincre, que ces révélations particuliers qui semblent accuser la Divinité d'une partialité facheuse pour quelqu'uns de ses créatures? Le tout-puissant n'auroit-il done pas des moyens plus convinqu ans de se montrer aux hornrnes que ces métamorphoses ridicules, ces incarnations prétendues, qui nous sont attestées par des écrivains si pen d'accord entre eux dans les récits qu'ils en font? Au lieu de tant de miracles, inventés pour prouver la mission divine de tant de législateurs, révérés par les differens peuples du monde, le souverain des esprits ne pouvoit-il pas convaincre tout d'un coup l'esprit humain des choses qu'il a voulu lui faire connoître? Au lieu de suspendre un soleil dans la voùte du firmament; an lieu de repandre sans ordre les étoiles, et les constellations qui remplissent l'espace, n'eut-il pas été plus conforme aux vues d'un Dieu si jaloux de sa gloire et si bien intentionné pour l'homme; d'ecrire d'une façon non sujette à dispute, son nom, ses attributs, ses volontés permanentes, en caracteres ineffaçables, et lisibles également pour tous les habitants de la terre? Personne alors n'auroit pu douter de l'existence d'un Dieu, de ses volontés claires, de ses intentions visibles. Sous les yeux de cc Dieu si terrible, personne n'auroit eu l'audace de violer ses ordonnances; nul rnortel n'eât osé se mettre dans le cas d'attirer sa colère: enfin nul homme n'eût en le front d'en imposer en son nom, ou d'interpréter ses volontés suivant ses propres phantasies. En effet, quand même on admetteroit l'existence du Dieu théologique, et la realité des attributs si discordans

112

qu'on lui donne, l'on ne pent en rien conclure, pour autoriser la conduite ou les cultes qu'on prescrit de lui rendre. La théologie est vraiment le tonneau des Danaides. A force de qualities contradictoires et d'as sertions hazardées, eile a, pour ainsi dire, tellement garoté son Dieu qu'elle a mis dans l'impossibilité d'agir. S'il est infiniment bon quelle raison aurions-nous de le craindre? S'il est infiniment sage, de quoi nous inquieter sur notre sort? S'il sait tout, pourquoir l'avertir de nos besoins, et le fatiguer de nos prières? S'il est partout, pourquoi lui élever des temples? S'il est maître de tout, pourquoi lui faire des sacrifices et des offrandes? S'il est juste, comment croire qu'il punisse des créatures qu'il a rempli des foiblesses? Si la grace fait tout en elles, quelle raison auroit-il de les recompenser? S'il est tout-puissant, comment l'offenser, comment lui resister? S'il est raisonnable, comment se mettroit-il en colèe contre des aveugles, à qui il a laissé la liberté de déraisonner? S'il est inamuable, dc quel droit pretendrions- nous faire changer ses decrets? S'il est inconcevable, pourquoi nous en occuper? S'IL A PARLE[d], POURQUOI L'UNIVERS N'EST-IL PAS CONVA1NCU? Si la connoissance d'un. Dieu est la plus nécessaire, pourquoi n'est-elle pas la plus évidente, et la plus claire.
-Systène de la Nature, London, 1781.

The enlightened and benevolent Pliny thus publicly professes himself an atheist:—Quapropter effigiem Dei, formainque quwrere, imbecillitatis humanæ reor. Quisquis est Deus (si modo est alius) et quacunque in parte, totus est sensus, totus est visus, totus auditus, totus animæ, totus anirni, totus sui. * * * * *
Imperfectæ vero in homine naturæ præcipua solatia ne deum quidem posse omnia. Namque nec sibi potest mortem consciscere, si velit, quod homini dedit optimum in tantis vitze pœnis: nec mortales æternitate donare, aut revocare defunctos; nee facere ut qui vixit non vixerit, qui honores gessit non gesserit, uullumque babere in præteritum jus, przeterquam oblivionis, atque (ut facetis quoque argumentis societas bæc cum deo copuletur) ut bis dena viginta non sint, et multa similiter etlicere non posse.—Per gum,

declaratur baud dubie, naturæ potentiam id quoque esse, quod Deum vocamus[e].—Plin. Nat. Ms. cap. de Deo.

The consistent Newtonian is necessarily an atheist. See Sir W. Drummond's Academical Questions, chap. iii.—Sir W. seems to consider the atheism to which it leads, as a sufficient presumption of the falsehood of the system of gravitation: bit surely it is more consistent with the good faith of philosophy to admit a deduction from facts, than an hypothesis incapable of proof, although it might militate with the obstinate preconceptions of the mob. Had this author, instead of inveighing against the guilt and absurdity of atheism, demonstrated its falsehood, his conduct would have been more suited to the modesty of the sceptic, and the toleration of the philosopher. Omnia enim per Bei potentiam facta sunt: imo, quia natura potentia nulla est nisi ipsa Bei potentia, autem est nos eatenus Bei potentiam non intelligere, quatenus causas naturales ignoramus; adeoque stulte ad eandem Bei potentiam recurritur, quando rei alienjus, causam naturalem, sive est, ipsam Bei potentiam ignora mus[f]. Spinosa, Tract. Theologico-Pol. chap. i. p. 14.

---[a] The burthen of proof.
[b] I do not invent hypothesis ; for whatever is not deduced from phcenomena,
is to be called an hypothesis; and hypotheses, either metaphysical or physical, or grounded on occult qualities, should not be allowed any room in philosophy.
[c] To tell what he is, you must be himself
[d] The primary theology of man made him first fear and worship even the elements gross and material objects, he then paid his adorations to the presiding agents of the elements, to inferior genii, to heroes, or to men endowed with great qualities. By continuing to reflect he thought to simplify things, by submitting all nature to a single agent, to a spirit, to an universal soul, which put this nature, nature, and its parts into motion. In ascending from cause, to cause, mankind have ended, by seeing nothing, and it is in the

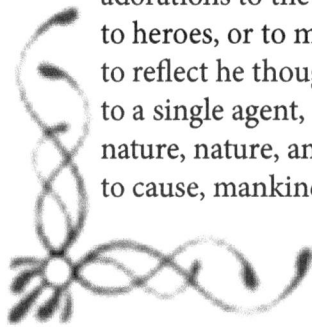

114

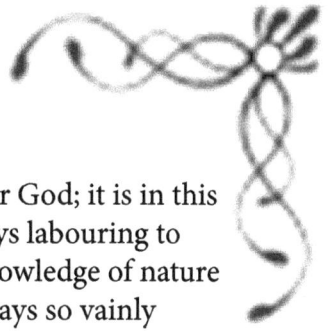

midst of this obscurity, that they have placed their God; it is in this dark abyss, that their restless imagination is always labouring to form clihneras, which will afflict them, until a knowledge of nature shall dissipate the phantoms which they have always so vainly adored. If we wish to render an account to ourselves, of our ideas respecting the Deity, we shall be obliged to confess that by the word God, men have never been able to designate any thing else hut the most hidden, the most remote, the most unknown cause of the effects which they perceive; they only make use of this word, when the springs of natural and known causes Lease to be visible to them; the instant they lose the thread, or their understanding can no longer follow the chain of these causes, they cut the knot of their difficulty and terminate their researches by calling God the last of these causes, that is to say, that which is beyond all the causes with which they are acquainted. Thus they, merely assign a vague denomination to an unknown cause, at which their indolence or the limits of their information compels them to stop. Whenever we are told, that God is the author of any phenomenon, that signifies that we are ignorant how such a phenomenon can be produced, with the assistance only of the natural powers or causes with which we are acquainted. It is thus that the generality of mankind, whose lot is ignorance, attribute to the Deity, not only the uncommon effects which strike them, but even the most simple events,-whose causes are the most easily discoverable, to all who have had the opportunity of reflecting on them. In a word man has always respected the unknown causes of those surprising effects, which his ignorance prevented him from unravelling. It was upon the ruins of nature that men first raised the imaginary colossus of a Deity If the ignorance of nature gave birth to gods, a knowledge of nature is calculated to destroy them. In proportion as man becomes informed, his powers and resources increase with his knowledge, the sciences, the conservative arts, and industry furnish him with assistance, experience inspires him with confidence, or procures him the means of resisting the efl'or(s of many causes, which cease to alarm him, as soon as he becomes

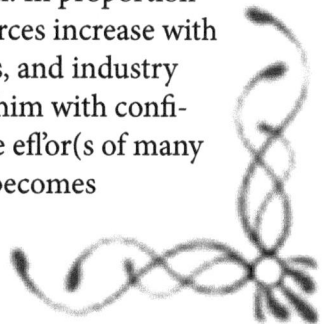

aquainted with them. In a word, his terrors are dissipated in the same proportion as his mind is enlightened. A well infoimed man ceases to be superstitious. It is never but on trust, that whole nations worship the God of their fathers, and their priests ; authority, confidence, submission, and custom, to them supply the place of proofs and conviction ; they prostrate themselves and pray, because their fathers have taught them to prostrate themselves and pray, but wherefore did the latter kneel? Because in remote periods, their guides and regulators, taught them it was a duty. "Worship and believe," said they "gods which you cannot comprehend, rely on our pinfound wisdom, we know more than you concerning the Deity." "But why should I rely on you ?" "Because it is the will of God, because he will punish you if you dare to resist." "But is not this God the thing in question?" Thus men have always been satisfied with this vicious circle, the indolence of their minds led them to believe the shorter mode was to rely upon the opinions of others. All religious notions, are founded upon authority alone, all the religions of the world forbid investigation, and will not permit reasoning; it is authority which requires us to believe in God, this God himself is only founded upon the authority of some men, who pretend to know him, and to be sent by bins to announce him to the world. A God made by men has doubtless need of men to snake him known to men. Is it then only, for the priests of the inspired, for metaphysicians, that a conviction of the existence of a God is reserved, and which is nevertheless said to be necessary to all mankind. But do we find a harmony of theological opinion among the inspired, or the reflective, in the different parts of the world? Are those even who profess to worship the same God agreed respecting him ? Are they satisfied with the proofs of his existence which their colleagues bring forward? Do they unanimously subscribe to the ideas which they adduce respecting his nature, his conduct, and the mode of understanding his pretended oracles? Is there a country, throughout the. earth in which the knowledge of God is really perfected. Has it assumed in any quarter the consistency, and uniformity, which we percieve human

116

knowledge to have assumed, in the most trifling arts, in trades the most despised. The words spirit, immateriality, creation, predestination, grace, this croud of subtile distinctions with which theology, in some countries, is universally filled, these ingenious inventions, imagined by the successive reasoners of ages, have, alas! only embroiled the question, and never has the science, the most important to mankind, been able to acquire the least stability. For thousands of years, have these idle dreamers transmitted to each other, the task of meditating on the Deity, of discovering his secret paths, of inventing hypotheses calculated to solve this important enigma. The little success they have met with, has not discouraged theological vanity. God has always been talked of, mankind have cut each others throats for him, and this great being still continues, to be the moat unknown, and the most sought after. Fortunate would it have been for mankind if confining themselves to the visible objects in which they are interested, they had employed in perfecting true science, laws, morals, and education, half the exertions they have made in their researches after a Deity. They would have been still wiser and more fortunate, could they have resolved to leave their blind guides to quarrel among themselves and to sound the depths calculated only to turn their brains without meddling with their senseless disputes. but it is the very essence of ignorance to attach importance to what it does not understand. Human vanity is such that the mind became irritated by difficulty. In proportion as an object fades from our sight do we exert ourselves to seize it, because it then stimulates our pride, it excites our curiosity and becomes interesting. In contending for his God every one in fact is only contending for the interests of his own vanity, which of all the passions, produced by the mal-organization of society, is the most prompt to take alarm, and the most calculated to give birth, to great absurdities. If laying aside for a moment the gloomy ideas which theology gives us of a capricious God, whose partial and despotic decrees decide the fates of men, we fix our eyes upon the pretended goodness which all men, even whilst trembling before this God, agree in giving to him, if we suppose him to be actuated

117

by the project which is attributed to him, of having only laboured for his own glory, of exacting the adoration of intelligent beings, of seeking only ii his works, the welfare of the human race; how can we reconcile his views and dispositions with the truly invincible ignorance in which this God so good and glorious leaves the greater part of mankind respecting himself? If God wishes to be known, beloved, and praised, why does he not reveal himself under some favourable features, to all those intelligent beings by whom he wishes to be loved and worshipped! Why does he not manifest to all the earth in an unequivocal manner, much more calculated to convince us, than by these particular revelations which seem to accuse the Deity of an unjust partiality for some of his creatures. Would not the Omnipotent possess more convincing means of revealing himself to mankind than these ridiculous metamorphoses, these pretended incarnations, which are attested to us by writers who so little agree among themselves in the recitals they give of them? Instead of so many mitacles invented to prove the divine mission of so many legislators revered by the different nations of the world, could hot the Supreme Being convince in an instant the human mind of the

things which he chose to make known to it? Instead of suspending the sun in the vault of the firmament, instead of dispersing the stars and the constellations, which occupy space without order, would it not have been more conformable to the views of a God so jealous of his glory, and so well disposed to man, to write in a mode not liable to be disputed, his name, his attributes, and his unchangeable will, in everlasting characters, equally legible to all the inhabitants of the earth? No one could then have doubted the existence of a God, his manifest will, his visible intentions, Under the eye of this terrible Deity, no one would have had the audacity to violate his ordinances, no mortal would have dared to place himself in the situation of drawing down his wrath ; and, lastly, no man would have had the effrontery to impose on his fellow creatures, in the name of the Deity, or to interpret his will according to his own fancy. In fact, even should the existence of the theological

God be admitted, and the reality of the discordant attributes which
are given to hirn, nothing could be inferred from it, to authorise
the conduct or the modes of worship, which we are told to observe
towards him. Theology is truly the tub of the Danaides.

By dint of contradictory qualities and rash assertions, it has so
trammelled, as it were, its God, that it has made it impossible for
him to act. If he is infinitely good, what reason have we to fear
him? If he is infinitely wise, why should we be uneasy for our
future state? If he knows all, why inform him of our wants, and
tease him with our prayers? If he is omn ipresent, why raise tem-
ples to him ? If he is master of all, why sacrifice and make ofierings
to bins? If he is just, how cau we believe that he punishes creatures
whom he has afflicted with weaknesses? If grace does all in them,
for what reason should he reward them ? If he is omnipotent how
can we offend, how resist hint? If he is reasonable, bow could be be
incensed against his blind creatures, to whom he has only left the
liberty of falling into error? If he is immutable, by what right do we
pretend to make him change his decrees? If he is incomprehensi-
ble, why do we busy ourselves in endeavouring to understand him?
If HE HAS SPOKEN, WHY IS NOT THE UNIVEESE CON-
VINCED? If the knowledge of a God is the most necessary, why
is not the clearest and most evident ?--Systent of Nat arc, Louclan,
1781.

^e For which reason, I consider that the inquiry after the form and
figure of the Deity, must be attributed to human weakness. What-
ever Gjd may be (if indeed there be one) and wherever he may
exist, he must be all sense, all sight, all hearing, all life, all mind,
self-existent. ***********

But it is a great consolation to man with all his infirmities to reflect
that God himself cannot do all things : for he cannot inflict on
himself death, even if he should wish to die, that best of gifts to
man amidst the cares and sufferings of life ; neither can he make
men eternal, nor raise the dead, nor prevent those who have lived
from living, nor those who have borne honours from wearing

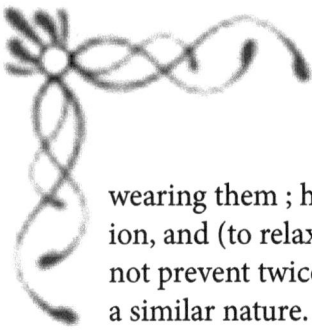

wearing them ; he has no power over the past, except that of obliv-
ion, and (to relax our gravity awhile and indulge in a joke) he can-
not prevent twice ten from being twenty, and many other things of
a similar nature. From these observations it is clearly apparent that
the powers of nature are what we call GA. Plin. Nat. Hist.

[f] All things are made by the power of God, yet, doubtless, because
the power of nature is the power of God : besides we are unable to
understand the power of God, so far as we are ignorant of natural
causes; therefore we foolishly recur to the power of God whenev-
er we are unacquainted with the natural cause of any thing, or in
other words, with the power of God.—Spinosa, Tract. Theologici.
Pol. chap. i. p. 14.

VII. PAGE 63.
Ahasuerus, rise !

Ahasuerus the Jew crept forth from the dark cave of Mount Carm-el. Near two thousand years have elapsed since he was first goaded by never-ending restlessness, to rove the globe from pole to pole. When out Lord was wearied with the burthen of his pounderous cross, and wanted to rest before the door of Ahasuerus, the unfeel-ing wretch staggered, sinking under the heavy load, but uttered no complaint. An angel of death appeared before Ahasuerus, and ex-claimed indignantly, "Barbarian! Thou hast denied rest to the Son of Man: be it denied thee also, until he comes to judge the world." A black demon, let loose from hell upon Ahasuerus, goads him now from country to country; he is denied the consolation which death affords, and precluded from the rest of the peaceful grave. Ahasuerus crept forth from the dark cave of Mount Carmel—he shook the dust from his beard—and taking up one of the sculls heaped there, hurled it down the eminence: it rebounded fromm the earth in shivered atoms. This was my father! roared Ahasuerus. Seven more sculls rolled down from rock to rock; while the infuri-ate Jew, following them with ghastly looks exclaimed— And these were my wives! He still continued to hurt down scull after scull, roaring in dreadful accents—And these, and these, and these were my children! They could die; but, I! reprobate wretch, alas! I can-not die! Dreadful beyond conception is the judgment that hangs over me. Jerusalem fell—I crushed the sucking babe, and precipi-tated myself into the destructive flames. I cursed the Romans— but, alas! alas! the restless curse held me by the hair, —and I could not die! Rome the giantess fell—I placed myself before the falling statue—she fell, and did not crush me. Nations sprung up and disappeared before me,--but I remained and did not die. From cloud-encircled cliffs did I precipitate myself into the ocean; but the foaming billows cast me upon the shore, and the burning arrow of existence pierced my cold heart again. I leaped into Etna's flaming abyss, and roared with the giants for ten long months,

The volcano fermented, and in a fiery stream of lava cast me up. I lay torn by the torture snakes of hell amid the glowing cinders, and yet continued to exist. A forest was on fire: I darted on wings of fury and despair into the crackling wood. Fire dropped upon me from the trees, but the flames only singed my limbs; alas! it could not consume them.—I now mixed with the butchers of mankind, and plunged in the tempest of the raging battle. I roared defiance to the infuriate Gaul, defiance to the victorious German; but arrows and spears rebounded in shivers from my body. The Saracen's flaming sword broke upon my scull: balls in vain hissed upon me: the lightnings of battle glared harmless around my loins: in vain did the elephant elephant trample on me, in vain the iron hoof of the wrathful steed! The mine, big with destructive power, burst upon me, and hurled me high in the air—I fell on heaps of smoking limbs, but was only singed. The giant's steel club rebounded from my body; the executioner's hand could not strangle me; the tyger's tooth could not pierce me, nor would the hungry lion in the circus devour me. I cohabited with poisonous snakes, and pinched the red crest of the dragon. The serpent stung, but could not destroy me;—the dragon tormented, but dared not to devour me. I now provoked the fury of tyrants: I said to Nero, Thou art a bloodhound! I said to Christiern, Thou art a bloodhound! I said to Muley Ismail, Thou art a bloodhound!—The tyrants invented cruel torments, but did not kill me.—Ha! not to be able to die—not to be able to die—not to be permitted to rest after the toils of life—to be doomed to be imprisoned for ever in the clay-formed dungeon—to be for ever clogged with this worthless body, its load of diseases and infirmities—to be condemned to hold for milenniums that yawning monster Sameness and Time, that hungry hyena, ever bearing children, and ever devouring again her offspring!—Ha! not to be permitted to die! Awful avenger in heaven, bast thou in thine armoury of wrath a punishment more dreadful? then let it thunder upon me, command, a hurricane to sweep me down to the foot of Carmel, that I there may lie extended; may pant, and writhe, and die! This fragment is the translation of part of some

some German work, whose title I have vainly endeavoured to discover. I picked it up, dirty and torn, some years ago, in Lincoln's-Inn Fields.

VII. PAGE 66.
I will beget a Son, and he ,shall bear
The sins of all the world.

A book is put into our hands when children, called the Bible, the purport of whose history is briefly this: That God made the earth in six days, and there planted a delightful garden, in which he placed the first pair of human beings. In the midst of the garden he planted a tree, whose fruit, although within their reach, they were forbidden to touch. That the Devil, in the shape of a snake, persuaded them to eat of this fruit; in consequence of which God condemned both them and their posterity yet unborn to satisfy his justice by their eternal misery. — — — — The book states, in addition, that the soul of whoever disbelieves his sacrifice will be burned with everlasting fire. During many ages of misery and darkness this story gained implicit belief; but at length men arose who suspected that it was a fable and imposture, and that Jesus Christ, so far from being a God, was only a man like themselves. But a numerous set of men, who derived and still derive immense emoluments from this opinion, in the shape of a popular belief, told the vulgar, that, if they did not believe in the Bible, they would be damned to all eternity; and burned, imprisoned, and poisoned all the unbiassed and unconnected enquirers who occasionally arose. They still oppress them, so far as the people, now become more enlightened, will allow. The belief in all that the Bible contains, is called Christianity. A Roman Governor of Judea, at the instance of a priest-led mob, crucified a man called Jesus eighteen centuries ago. He was a man of pure life, who desired to rescue his countrymen from the tyranny of their barbarous and degrading superstitions. The common fate of all who desire to benefit mankind awaited him. The rabble, at the instigation of the priests,

123

demanded his death, although his very judge made public acknowledgment of his innocence. Jesus was sacrificed to the honour of that God with whom he was afterwards confounded. It is of importance, therefore to distinguish between the pretended character of this being, as the Son of God and the Saviour of the world, and his real character as a man, who, for a vain attempt to reform the world, paid the forfeit of his life to that Overbearing tyranny which has since so long desolated the universe in his name. Whilst the one, who announces himself as the God of compassion and peace — — — — — the other stands in the foremost list of those true heroes, who have died in the glorious martyrdom of liberty, and have braved torture, contempt, and poverty, in the cause of suffering humanity[a]. The vulgar, ver in extremes, became persuaded that the crucifixion of Jesus was a supernatural event. Testimonies of miracles, so frequent in unenlightened ages, were not wanting to prove that he was something divine. This belief, rolling through the lapse of ages, met with the reveries of Plato and the reasonings of Aristotle, and acquired force and extent, until The divinity of Jesus became a dogma, which to dispute was death, which to doubt was infamy. Christianity is now the established religion: he who attempts to impugn it, must be contented to behold murderers and traitors take precedence of him in public opinion; though, if his genius be equal to his courage, and assisted by a peculiar coalition of circumstances, future ages may exalt him to a divinity, and persecute others in his name, as he was persecuted in the name of his predecessor in the homage of the world. The same means that have supported every other popular belief, have supported Christianity. War, imprisonment, assassination, and falsehood; deeds of unexampled and incomparable atrocity have made it what it is. The blood shed by the votaries of the God of mercy and peace, since the establishment of his religion, would probably suffice to drown all other sectaries now on the habitable globe. We derive from our ancestors a faith thus fostered and supported: we quarrel, persecute, and hate for its maintenance. Even under a government which, whilst it infringes the very right of thought and speech,

124

boasts of permitting the liberty of the press, a man is pilloried and imprisoned because he is a Deist, and no one raises his voice in the indignation of outraged humanity. But it is ever a proof that the falsehood of a proposition is felt by those who use coercion, not reasoning, to procure its admission; and a dispassionate observer would feel himself more powerfully interested in favour of a man, who, depending on the truth of his opinions, simply stated his reasons for entertaining them, than in that of his aggressor, who, daringly avowing his unwillingness or incapacity to answer them by argument, proceeded to repress the energies and break the spirit of their promulgator by that torture and imprisonment whose infliction he could command. Analogy seems to favour the opinion, that as, like other systems, Christianity has arisen and augmented, so like them it will decay and perish; that, as violence, darkness, and deceit, not reasoning and persuasion, have procured its admission among mankind, so, when enthusiasm has subsided, and time, that infallible controverter of false opinions, has involved its pretended evidences in the darkness of antiquity, it will become obsolete; that Milton's poem alone will give permanency to the remembrance of its absurdities; and that men will laugh as heartily at grace, faith, redemption, and original sin, as they now do at the metamorphoses of Jupiter, the miracles of Romish saints, the efficacy of witchcraft, and the appearance of departed spirits. Had the Christian religion commenced and continued by the mere force of reasoning and persuasion, the preceding analogy would be inadmissible. We should never speculate on the future obsoleteness of a system perfectly conformable to nature and reason: it would endure so long as they endured; it would be a truth as indisputable as the light of the sun, the criminality of murder, and other facts, whose evidence, depending on our organization and relative situations, must remain acknowledged as satisfactory, so long as man is mau. It is an incontrovertible fact, the consideration of which ought to repress the hasty conclusions of credulity, or moderate its obstinacy in maintaining them, that, had the Jews not been a fanatical race of men, had even the resolution of Pontius Pilate been equal to his candour, the Christian religion never could have prevailed, it could not even have existed: on so feeble a thread hangs the most cherished opinion of a sixth of the human race! When will the vulgar learn humility? When will the pride of ignorance blush at having believed before it could comprehend? Either the Christian religion is true, or it is false: if true, it conies from God, and its authenticity can admit of doubt and dispute no further than its omnipotent author is willing to allow. Either the power or the goodness of God is called in question, if he leaves those doctrines most essential to the well being of man in doubt and dispute; the only ones which, since their promulgation have been the subject of unceasing cavil, the cause of irreconcileable hatred. If God has spoken, why is not the universe convinced? There is this passage in the Christian Scriptures: "Those who obey not God, and believe not the Gospel of his Son, shall be punished with everlasting destruction." This is the pivot upon which all religions turn: they all assume that it is in our power to believe or not to believe; whereas the mind can only believe that which it thinks true. A human being can only be supposed accountable for those actions which are influenced by his will. But belief is utterly distinct from and unconnected with volition: it is the apprehension of the agreement or disagreement of the ideas that compose any proposition. Belief is a passion, or involuntary operation of the mind, and, like other passions, its intensity is precisely proportionate to the degrees of excitement. Volition is essential to merit or demerit. But the Christian religion attaches the highest possible degrees of merit and demerit to that which is worthy of neither, and which is totally unconnected with the peculiar faculty of the mind, whose presence is essential to their being. Christianity was intended to reform the world: had an all-wise Being planned it, nothing is more improbable than that it should have failed: omniscience would infallibly have foreseen the inutility of a scheme which experience demonstrates, to this age, to have been utterly unsuccessful. Christianity inculcates the necessity of supplicating the Deity. Prayer ay be considered under two points of view; as an endeavour to

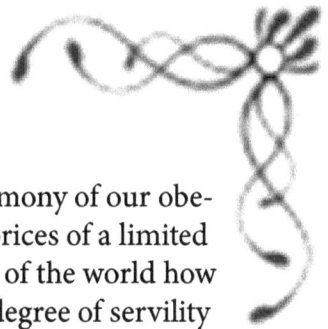

change the intentions of God, or as a formal testimony of our obe-
dience. But the former case supposes that the caprices of a limited
intelligence can occasionally instruct the Creator of the world how
to regulate the universe; and the latter, a certain degree of servility
analogous to the loyalty demanded by earthly tyrants. Obedience
indeed is only the pitiful and cowardly egotism of him who thinks
that he can do something better than reason. Christianity, like all
other religions, rests upon miracles, prophesies, and martyrdoms.
No religion ever existed, which had not its prophets, its attested
miracles, and, above all, crowds of devotees who would bear pa-
tiently the most horrible tortures to prove its authenticity. It should
appear that in no case can a discriminating mind subscribe to the
genuineness of a miracle. A miracle is an infraction of nature's law,
by a supernatural cause; by a cause acting beyond that eternal
circle within which all things are included. God breaks through
the law of nature, that he may convince mankind of the truth of
that revelation which, in spite of his precautions, has been, since is
introduction, the subject of unceasing schism and cavil. Miracles
resolve themselves into the following question[b]:— Whether it is
more probable the laws of nature, hitherto so immutably harmoni-
ous, should have undergone violation, or that a man should have
told a lie? Whether it is more probable that we are ignorant of the
natural cause of an event, or that we know the supernatural one?
That, in old times, when the powers of nature were less known
than at present, a certain set of men were themselves deceived, or
had some hidden motive for deceiving others; or that God begat a
son, who, in his legislation, measuring merit by belief, evidenced
himself to be totally ignorant of the powers of the human mind—
of what is voluntary, and what is the contrary? We have many in-
stances of men telling lies;—none of an infraction of nature's laws,
those laws of whose government alone we have any knowledge or
experience. The records of all nations afford innumerable instances
of men deceiving others either from vanity or interest, or them-
selves being deceived by the limitedness of their views and their
ignorance of natural causes: but where is to life before our eyes,

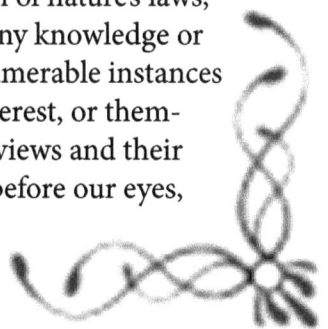

causes: but where is the accredited case of God having come upon earth, to give the lie to his own creations? There would be something truly wonderful in the appearance of a ghost; but the assertion of a child that he saw one as he passed through the churchyard, is universally admitted to be less miraculous. But even supposing that a man should raise a dead body to life before our eyes, and on this fact rest his claim to being considered the son of God;—the Humane Society restores drowned persons, and because it makes no mystery of the method it employs, its members are not mistaken for the sons of God. All that we have a right to infer from our ignorance of the cause of any event is that we do not know it: had the Mexicans attended to this simple rule when they heard the cannon of the Spaniards, they would not have considered them as gods: the experiments of modern chemistry would have defied the wisest philosophers of ancient Greece and Rome to have accounted for them on natural principles. An author of strong common sense has observed, that. "a miracle is no miracle at second-hand;" he might have added, that a miracle is no miracle in any case; for until we are acquainted with all natural causes, we have no reason to imagine others. There remains to be considered another proof of Christianity—Prophecy. A book is written before a certain event, in which this event is foretold; how could the prophet have foreknown it without inspiration? how could he have been inspired Without God? The greatest stress is laid on the prophecies of Moses and Hosea on the dispersion of the Jews, and that of Isaiah concerning the coining of the Messiah. The prophecy of Moses is a collection of every possible cursing and blessing; and it is so far from being marvellous that the one of dispersion should have been fulfdled, that it would have been more surprising if, out of all these, none should have taken effect. In Deuteronomy, chap. xxviii. ver. 64, where Moses explicitly foretells the dispersion, he states that they shall there serve gods of wood and stone: " And the Lord shall scatter thee among all people, from the one end of the earth even to the other, and there thou shalt serve other gods, which neither thou nor thy fathers have known, even gods of and stone." The Jews are at this day remarkably tenacious of their religion. Moses also declares that they shall be subjected to these causes for disobedience to his ritual: " And it shall come to pass, if thou will not hearken unto the voice of the Lord thy God, to observe to do all the commandments and statutes which I command you this day, that all these curses shall come upon thee and overtake thee." Is this the real reason? The third, fourth and fifth chapters of Hosea are a piece of immodest confession. The indelicate type might apply in a hundred senses to a hundred things. The fifty-third chapter of Isaiah is more explicit, yet it does not exceed in clearness the oracles of Delphos. The historical proof, that Moses, Isaiah and Hosea did write when they are said to have written, is far from being clear and circumstantial. But prophecy requires proof in its character as a miracle; we have no right to suppose that a man foreknew future events from God, until it is demonstrated that he neither could know them by his own exertions, nor that the writings which contain the prediction could possibly have been fabricated after the event pretended to be foretold. It is more probable that writings, pretending to divine inspiration, should have been fabricated after the fulfilment of their pretended prediction, than that they should have really been divinely inpired; when we consider that the latter supposition makes God at once the creator of the human mind and ignorant of its primary powers, particularly as we have numberless instances of false religions, and forged prophesies of things long past, and no accredited case of God having conversed with men directly or indirectly. It is also possible that the description of an event might have foregone its occurrence; but this is far from being a legitimate proof of a divine revelation, as many men, not pretending to the character of a prophet, have nevertheless, in this sense, prophesied. Lord Chesterfield was never yet taken for a prophet, even by a bishop, yet he uttered this remarkable prediction: "The despotic government of France is screwed up to the highest pitch; a revolution is fast approaching; that revolution, I am convinced, will be radical and sanguinary." This appeared in the letters of the prophet long before the accomplishment of this wonderful prediction. Now, have these particulars come to pass, or have they not? If they have, how could the Earl have foreknown them without inspiration? If we admit the truth of the Christian religion on testimony such as this, we must admit, on the same strength of evidence, that God has affixed the highest rewards to belief, and the eternal tortures of the never-dying worm to disbelief; both of which have been demonstrated to be involuntary. The last proof of the Christian religion depends on the influence of the Holy Ghost. Theologians divide the influence of the Holy Ghost into its ordinary and extraordinary modes of operation. The latter is supposed to be that which inspired the Prophets and Apostles; and the former to be the grace of God, which summarily makes known the truth of his revelation, to those whose mind is fitted for its reception by a submission perusal of his word. Persons convinced in this manner, can do any thing but account for their conviction, describe the time at which it happened, or the manner in which it came upon them. It is supposed to enter the mind by other channels than those of the senses, and therefore professes to be superior to reason founded on their experience. Admitting, however, the usefulness or possibility of a divine revelation, unless we demolish the foundations of all human knowledge, it is requisite that our reason should previously demonstrate its genuineness; for, before we extinguish the steady ray of reason and common sense, it is fit that we should discover whether we cannot do without their assistance, whether or no there be any other which may suffice to guide us through the labyrinth of life[c]: for, if a man is to be inspired upon all occasions, if he is to be sure of a thing because he is sure, if the ordinary operations of the spirit are not to be considered very extraordinary modes of demonstration, if enthusiasm is to usurp the place of proof, and madness that of sanity, all reasoning is superfluous. The Mahometan dies fighting for his prophet, the Indian immolates himself at the chariot-wheels of Brahma, the Hottentot worships an insect, the Negro a bunch of feathers, the Mexican sacrifices human victims! Their degree of conviction must certainly be very

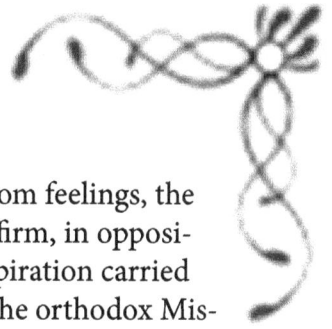

strong: it cannot arise from conviction, it must from feelings, the reward of their prayers. If each of these should affirm, in opposition to the strongest possible arguments, that inspiration carried internal evidence, I fear their inspired brethren, the orthodox Missionaries, would be so uncharitable as to pronounce them obstinate. Miracles cannot be received as testimonies of a disputed fact, because all human testimony has ever been insufficient to establish the possibility of miracles. That which is incapable of proof itself, is no proof of any thing else. Prophecy has also been rejected by the test of reason. Those, then, who have been actually inspired, are the only true believers in the Christian religion.

Mox numine viso
Virginei tumuere sinus, irmuptaque mater
Arcano stupuit compleri viscera partu
Auctorum paritura suum. Mortalia corda
Artificem texere poli, latuitque sub uno
Pectore, qui totum late complectitur orbem.
Claudian, Carmen Pasehale.[d]

----[a] Since writing this note I have seen reason to suspect, that Jesus was an ambitious man, who aspired to the throne of Judea,
[b] See Hume's Essay, vol. H. page 121.
[c] See Locke's Essay on the HMI-Ian Understanding, book iv. chap. ix., on Enthusiasm.
[d] Upon seeing the Divinity, the Virgin's womb soon swelled, and the unmarried mother was amazed to find herself filled with a mysterious progeny, and that she was to bring forth to the world her own Creator. A mortal frame veiled the Framer of the Heavens, and he who embraces the wide surrounding circle of the world, lay himsclf concealed in the recesses of the womb.

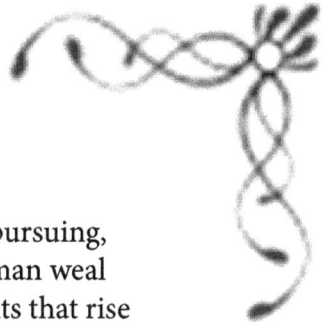

VIII. PAGE 79.

Him, (still from hope to hope the bliss pursuing,
Which, from the exhaustless lore of human weal
Dawns on the virtuous mind,) the thoughts that rise
In time-destroying infiniteness, gift
With self-enshrined eternity, &c.

Time is our consciousness of the succession of ideas in our mind. Vivid sensation, of either pain or pleasure, makes the time seem long, as the common phrase is, because it renders us more acutely conscious of our ideas. If a mind be conscious of an hundred ideas during one minute, by the clock, and of two hundred actually occupy so much greater extent in the mind as two exceed one in quantity. If, therefore, the human mind, by any future improvement of its sensibility, should become conscious of an infinite number of ideas in a minute, that minute would be eternity. I do not hence infer that the actual space between the birth and death of a man will ever be prolonged; but that his sensibility is perfectible, and that the number of 'ideas which his mind is capable of receiving is indefinite. One man is stretched on the rack during twelve hours; another sleeps soundly in his bed: the difference of time perceived by these two persons is immense; one hardly will believe that half an hour has elapsed, the other could credit that centuries had flown during his agony. Thus, the life of a man of virtue and talent, who should die in his thirtieth year, is, with regard to his own feelings, longer than that of a miserable priest-ridden slave, who dreams out a century of dulness. The one has perpetually cultivated his mental faculties, has rendered himself master of his thoughts, can abstract and generalize amid the lethargy of every-day business;— the other can slumber over the brightest moments of his being, and is unable to remember the happiest hour of his life. Perhaps the perishing epherneron enjoys a longer life than the tortoise.

Dark flood of time!
Roll as it listeth thee—I measure not
By months or moments thy ambiguous course.
Another may stand by me on the brink
And watch the bubble whirled beyond his ken
That pauses at my feet. The sense of love,
The thirst for action, and the impassioned thought
Prolong my being: if I wake no more,
My life more actual living will contain
Than some grey veterans' Of the world's cold school,
Whose listless hours unprofitably roll, -
By one enthusiast feeling unredeemed.
See Godwin's Pol. Jus. vol. i. page 411;— and Condorcet, Esquisse
d'un Tableau Historique des Progrs de l'Esprit Ilumain, Epoque i

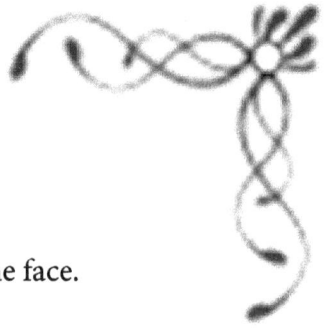

VIII. PAGE 79.

No longer now
He slays the lamb that looks him in the face.

I hold that the depravity of the physical and moral nature of man originated in his unnatural habits of life. The origin of man, like that of the universe of which he is a part, is enveloped in impenetrable mystery. His generations either had a beginning, or they had not. The weight of evidence in favour of each of these suppositions seems tolerably equal; and it is perfectly unimportant to the present argument which is assumed. The language spoken, however, by the mythology of nearly all religions seems to prove, that at some distant period man forsook the path of nature, and sacrificed the purity and happiness of his being to unnatural appetites. The date of this event seems to have also been that of some great change in the climates of the earth, with which it has an obvious correspondence. The allegory of Adam and Eve eating of the tree of evil, and entailing upon their posterity the wrath of God, and the loss of everlasting life admits of no other explanation than the disease and crime that have flowed from unnatural diet. Milton was so well aware of this,
that he makes Raphael thus exhibit to Adam the consequence of his disobedience.
--------------------Immediately a place
Before his eyes appeared: sad, noisome, dark:,
A lazar-house it seern'd; wherein were laid
Numbers of all diseased: all maladies
Of ghastly spasm, or racking torture, qualms
Of heart-sick agony, all feverous kinds,
Convulsions, epilepsies, fierce catarrhs,
Intestine stone and ulcer, cholic pangs,
DFemoniac frenzy, moping melancholy,
And moon-struck madness, pining atrophy,
Marasmus, and wide-wasting pestilence,
Dropsies, and asthmas, and joint-racking rheums.

And how many thousands more might not be added to this frightful catalogue!

The story of Prometheus is one like wise which, although universally admitted to be allegorical, has never been satisfactorily explained. Prometheus stole fire from heaven, and was chained for this crime to mount Caucasus, where a vulture continually devoured his liver, that grew to meet its hunger. Hesiod says, that, before the time of Prometheus, mankind were exempt from suffering; that they enjoyed a vigorous youth, and that death, when at length it came, approached like sleep, and gently closed their eyes. Again, so general was this opinion, that Horace, a poet of the Augustan age, writes—

> Audax omnia perpeti,
> Gens humana mit per vetitum nefas ;
> Audax Iapeti genus
> Ignem fraude mala gentibus intulit:
> Post ignem zetheria domo
> Subductum, macieset nova febrium
> Terris incubuit cohors,
> Semotique prius tarda necessitas
> Lethi corripuit gradum[a].

How plain a language is spoken by all this. Prometheus (who represents the human race) effected some great change in the condition of his nature, and applied fire to culinary purposes; thus inventing an expedient for screening from his disgust the horrors of the shambles, From this moment his vitals were devoured by the vulture of disease. It consumed his being in every shape of its loathsome and infinite variety, inducing the soul-quelling sinkings of premature and violent death. All vice arose from the ruin of healthful innocence. Tyranny, superstition, commerce, and inequality, were then first known, when reason vainly attempted to guide the wanderings of exacerbated 'passion. I conclude this part of the subject with an extract from Mr. Newton's Defence of

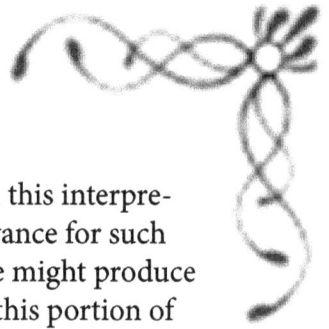

Vegetable Regimen, from whom I have borrowed this interpretation of the fable of Prometheus. " Making allowance for such transposition of the 'events of the allegory as time might produce after the important truths were forgotten, which this portion of the ancient mythology was intended to transmit, the drift of the fable seems to be this:—Man at his creation was endowed with the gift of perpetual youth; that is, be was not formed to be a sickly suffering creature as we now see him, but to enjoy health, and to sink by slow degrees into the bosom of his parent earth without disease or pain. Prometheus first taught the use of animal food (primus bovem occidit Prometheus[b]) and of fire, with which to render it more digestible and pleasing to the taste. Ju.piter, and the rest of the gods, foreseeing the consequences of these inventions, were amused or irritated at the short-sighted devices of the newly formed creature, arid left him to experience the sad effects of them. Thirst, the necessary concomitant of a flesh diet," (perhaps of all diet vitiated by culinary preparation,) ensued; water was resorted to, and man forfeited the inestimable gift of health which he had received from heaven: he became diseased, the partaker of a precarious existence, and no longer descended slowly to his grave.[c]"

> But just disease to luxury succeeds,
> And every death its own avenger breeds;
> The fury passions from that blood began,
> And turned on man a fiercer savage—man.

Man, and the animals whom he has infected with his society, or depraved by his dominion, are alone diseased. The wild hog, the mouflon, the bison, and the wolf, are perfectly exempt from malady, and invariably die either from external violence, or natural old age. But the domestic hog, the sheep, the cow, and the dog are, subject to an incredible variety of distempers; and, like the corrupters of their nature, have physicians who thrive upon their miseries. The supereminence of man is like Satan's, a supereminence of pain; and the majority of his species, doomed to penury,

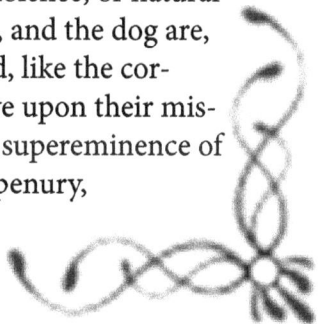

disease and, crime, have reason to curse the untoward event, that by enabling him to communicate his sensations, raised him above the level of his fellow animals. But the steps that have been taken are irrevocable. The whole of human science is comprised in one question:—How can the advantages of intellect and civilization be reconciled with the liberty and pure pleasures of natural life? How can we take the benefits, and reject the evils of the system, which is now interwoven with all the fibres of our being?-1. believe that abstinence from animal food and spirituous liquors would in a great measure capacitate us for the solution of this important question. Is it ture, that mental and bodily derangement is attributable in part to other deviations from rectitude and nature than those which concern diet. The mistakes cherished by society respecting the connection of the sexes, whence the misery and diseases of unsatisfied. celibacy, unenjoying prostitution, and the premature arrival of puberty necessarily spring; the putrid atmosphere of crowded cities; the exhalations of chemical processes; the muffling of our bodies in superfluous apparel; the absurd treatment of infants:—all these, and innumerable other causes, contribute their mite to the mass of human evil. Comparative anatomy teaches us that man resembles frugivorous animals in every thing, and carnivorous in nothing; he has neither claws wherewith to seize his prey, nor distinct and pointed teeth to tear the living fibre. A Mandarin of the first class, with nails two inches long, would probably find them alone, inefficient to hold even a hare. After every subterfuge of gluttony, the bull must be degraded into the ox, and the ram into the vvether, by an unnatural and inhuman operation, that the flaccid fibre may offer a fainter resistance to rebellious nature. It is only by softening and disguising dead flesh by culinary preparation, that it is rendered susceptible of mastication or digestion; and that the sight of its bloody juices and raw horror does not excite intolerable loathing and disgust. Let the advocate of animal food force himself to a decisive experiment on its fitness, and, as Plutarch recommends, tear a living lamb with his teeth, and plunging his head into its vitals, slake his thirst with the steaming blood;

138

when fresh from the deed of horror, let him revert to the irresistible instincts of nature that would rise in judgment against it, and say, Nature formed me for such work as this. Then, and then only, would he be consistent. Man resembles no carnivorous animal. There is no exception, unless man be one, to the rule of herbivorous animals having cellulated colons. The orang-outang perfectly resembles man both in the order and number of his teeth. The orang-outang is the most anthropomorphous of the ape tribe, all of which are strictly frugivorous. There is no other species of animals, which live on different food, in which this analogy exists[d]. In many frugivorous animals, the canine teeth are more pointed and distinct than those of man. The resemblance also of the human stomach to that of the orang-outang, is greater than to that of any other animal. The intestines are also identical with those of herbivorus animals, which present a larger surface for absorption and have ample and cellulate colons. The cœcum also, though short, is larger than that of carnivorous animals; and even here the orang-outang retains it's accustomed similarity. The structure of the human frame than is that of one fitted to a pure vegetable diet, in every essential particular. It is true, that the reluctance to abstain from animal food, in those who have been long accustomed to its stimulus, is so great in some persons of weak minds, as to be scarcely overcome; but this is far from bringing any argument in its favour. A lamb, which was fed for some time on flesh by a ship's crew, refused its natural diet at the end of the voyage. There are numerous instances of horses, sheep, oxen, and even wood-pigeons, having been taught to live upon flesh, until they have loathed their natural aliment. Young children evidently prefer pastry, oranges, apples, and other fruit, to the flesh of animals, until, by the gradual depravation of the digestive organs, the free use of vegetables has for a time produced serious inconveniences; for a time, I say, since there never was an instance wherein a change from spirituous liquors and animal food to vegetables and pure water, has failed ultimately to invigorate the body, by rendering its juices bland and consentaneous, and to restore to the mind that cheerfulness and

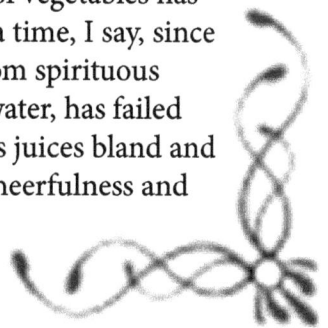

elasticity, which not one in fifty possesses on the present system. A love of strong liquors is also with difficulty taught to infants. Almost every one remembers the wry faces which the first glass of port produced. Unsophisticated instinct is invariably unerring; but to decide on the fitness of animal food, from the perverted appetites which its constrained adoption produces, is to make the criminal a judge in his own cause: it is even worse, it is appealing to the infatuated drunkard in a question of the salubrity of brandy. What is the cause of morbid action in the animal system? Not the air we breathe, for our fellow denizens of nature breathe the same uninjured; not the water we drink, (if remote from the pollutions of man and his inventions[e],) for the animals drink it too; not the earth we tread upon; not the unobscured sight of glorious nature, in the wood, the field, or the expanse of sky and ocean; nothing that we are or do in common with the undiseased inhabitants of the forest. Something then wherein we differ from them: our habit of altering our food by fire, so that our appetite is no longer a just criterion for the fitness of its gratification. Except in children there remain no traces of that instinct which determines, in all other animals, what aliment is natural or otherwise; and so perfectly obliterated are they in the reasoning adults of our species, that it has become necessary to urge considerations drawn from comparative anatomy, to prove that we are naturally frugivorous. Crime is madness. Madness is disease. Whenever the cause of disease shall be discovered, the root, from which all vice and misery have so long overshadowed the globe, will lie bare to the axe. All the exertions of man, from that moment, may be considered as tending to the clear profit of his species. No sane mind in a sane body resolves upon a real crime. It is a man of violent passions, blood-shot eyes, and swollen veins, that alone can grasp the knife of murder. The system of a simple diet promises no Utopian advantages. It is no mere reform of legislation, whilst the furious passions and evil propensities of the human heart, in which it had its origin, are still unassuaged. It strikes at the root of all evil, and is an experiment which may be tried with success, not alone by nations, but by small societies, families, and even individuals. In no eases has a return to vegetable diet produced the slightest injury; in most it has been attended with changes undeniably beneficial. Should ever a physician be born with the genius of Locke, I am persuaded that he might trace all bodily and mental derangements to our unnatural habits, as clearly as that philosopher has traced all knowledge to sensation. What prolific sources of disease are not those mineral and vegetable poisons that have been introduced for its extirpation! How many thousands have become murderers and robbers, bigots and domestic tyrants, dissolute and abandoned adventurers, from the use of fermented liquors; who had they slaked their thirst only with pure water, would have lived but to diffuse the happiness of their own unperverted feelings. How many groundless opinions and absurd institutions have not received a general sanction from the sottishness and intemperance of individuals! Who will assert that, had the populace of Paris satisfied their hunger at the ever-furnished table of vegetable nature, they would have lent their brutal suffrage to the proscription-list of Robespierre? Could a set of men, whose passions were not perverted by unnatural stimuli, look with coolness on an auto da Fè? Is it to be believed that a being of gentle feelings, rising from his meal of roots, would take delight in sports of blood? Was Nero a man of temperate life? Could you read calm health in his cheek, flushed with ungovernable propensities of hatred for the human race? Did Muley Ismael's pulse beat evenly, was his skin transparent, did his eyes beam with healthfulness, and its invariable concomitants, cheerfulness and benignity? Though history has decided none of these questions, a child could not hesitate to answer in the negative. Surely the bile-suffused cheek of Buonaparte, his wrinkled brow, and yellow eye, the ceaseless inquietude of his nervous system, speak no less plainly the character of his unresting ambition than his murders and his victories. It is impossible, had Buonaparte descended from a race of vegetable feeders, that he could have had either the inclination or the power to ascend the throne of the Bourbons. The desire of tyranny could scarcely be excited in the individual, the power to tyrannize would certainly not be delegated by a society-neither frenzied by inebriation, nor rendered impotent and irrational by disease. Pregnant indeed with inexhaustible calamity is the renunciation of instinct, as it concerns our physical nature; arithmetic cannot enumerate, nor reason perhaps suspect, the multitudinous sources of disease in civilized life. Even common water, that apparently innoxious pabulum, when corrupted by the filth of populous cities, is a deadly and insidious destroyer[f]. Who can wonder that all the inducements held out by God himself in the Bible to virtue should have been vainer than a nurse's tale; — — — — — — whilst Christians are in the daily practice of all those habits which have infected with disease and crime, not only the reprobate sons, but these favoured children of the common Father's love. Omnipotence itself could not save them from the consequences of this original and universal sin. There is no disease, bodily or mental, which adoption of vegetable diet and pure water has not infallibly mitigated, wherever the experiment has been fairly tried. Debility is gradually converted into strength, disease into healthfulness; madness, in all its hideous variety, from the ravings of the fettered maniac, to the unaccountable irrationalities of ill temper, that make a hell of domestic life, into a calm and considerate evenness of temper, that alone might offer a certain pledge of the future moral reformation of society. On a natural system of diet, old age would be our last and our only malady; the term of our existence would be protracted; we should enjoy life, and no longer preclude others from the enjoyment of it; all sensational delights would be infinitely more exquisite and perfect; the very sense of being would then be a continued pleasure, such as we now feel it in some few and favoured moments of our youth. By all that is sacred in our hopes for the human race, I conjure those who love happiness and truth, to give a fair trial to the vegetable system. Reasoning is surely superfluous on a subject whose merits an experience of six months would set for ever at rest. But it is only among the enlightened and benevolent that so great a sacrifice of appetite and prejudice can be expected, even though its ultimate excellence should not admit of dispute. It is found easier, by the short-sighted victims of disease, to palliate their torments by medicine, than to prevent them by regimen. The vulgar of all ranks are invariably sensual and indocile; yet I cannot but feel myself persuaded, that when the benefits of vegetable diet are mathematically proved; when it is as clear, that those who live naturally are exempt from premature death, as that nine is not one, the most sottish of mankind will feel a preference towards a long and tranquil, contrasted with a short and painful life. On the average, out of sixty persons, four die in three years, Hopes are entertained that in April 1814, a statement will be given that sixty persons, all having lived more than three years on vegetables and pure water, are then in perfect health. More than two years have now elapsed; not one of them has died; no such example will be found in any sixty persons taken at random. Seventeen persons of all ages (the families of Dr. Lambe and Mr. Newton) have lived for seven years on this diet without a death, and almost without the slightest illness. Surely, when we consider that some of these were infants, and one a martyr to asthma now nearly subdued, we may challenge any seventeen persons taken at random in this city to exhibit a parallel case. Those who may have been excited to question the rectitude of established habits of diet, by these loose remarks, should consult Mr. Newton's luminous and eloquent essay[g]. When these proofs come fairly before the world, and are clearly seen by all who understand arithmetic, it is scarcely possible that abstinence from aliments demonstrably pernicious should not become universal. In proportion to the Dumber of proselytes, so will be the weight of evidence; and when a thousand persons can be produced, living on vegetables and distilled water, who have to dread no disease but old age, the world will be compelled to regard animal flesh and fermented liquors as slow but certain poisons. The change which would be produced by simpler habits on political economy, is sufficiently remarkable. The monopolizing eater of animal flesh would no longer destroy his constitution by devouring an acre at a meal, and many loaves of bread would cease to contribute to gout, madness, and apoplexy, in the shape of a pint of porter, or a dram of gin, when appeasing the long-protracted famine of the hard-working peasant's hungry babes. The quantity of nutritious vegetable matter, consumed in fattening the carcase of an ox, would afford ten times the sustenance, undepraving indeed, and incapable of generating disease, if gathered immediately from the bosom of the earth.. The most fertile districts of the habitable globe are now actually cultivated by men for animals, at a delay and waste of aliment absolutely incapable of calculation. It is only the wealthy that can, to any great degree, even now, indulge the unnatural craving for dead flesh, and they pay for the greater licence of the privilege, by subjection to supernumerary diseases. Again, the spirit of the nation that should take the lead in this great reform, would insensibly become agricultural; commerce, with all its vice, selfishness, and corruption, would gradually decline; more natural habits would produce gentler manners, and the excessive complication of political relations would be so far simplified, that every individual might feel and understand why he loved his country, and took a personal interest in its welfare. How would England, for example, depend on the caprices of foreign rulers, if she contained within herself all the necessaries, and despised whatever they possessed of the luxuries of life? How could they starve her into compliance with their views? Of what consequence would it be that they refused to take her woollen manufactures, when large and fertile tracts of the island ceased to be allotted to the waste of pasturage? On a natural system of diet, we should require no spices from India; no wines from Portugal, Spain, France, or Madeira; none of those multitudinous articles of luxury, for which every corner of the globe is rifled, and which are the causes of so much individual rivalship, such calamitous and sanguinary national disputes. In the history of modern times, the avarice of commercial monopoly, no less than the ambition of weak and wicked chiefs, seems to have fomented the universal discord, to have added stubbornness to the mistakes of cabinets, and indocility to the infatuation of the people. Let it ever be remembered, that it is the direct influence of commerce

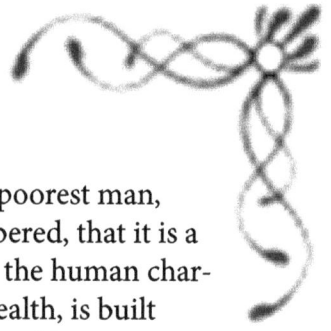

to make the interval between the richest and the poorest man, wider and more unconquerable. Let it be remembered, that it is a foe to every thing of real worth and excellence in the human character. The odious and disgusting aristocracy of wealth, is built upon the ruins of all that is good in chivalry or republicanism; and luxury is the forerunner of a barbarism scarce capable of cure. Is it impossible to realize a state of society, where all the energies of man shall be directed to the production of his solid happiness? Certainly, if this advantage (the object of all political speculation) be in any degree attainable, it is attainable only by a community, which holds out no factitious incentives to the avarice and ambition of the few, and which is internally organized for the liberty, security, and comfort of the many. None must be entrusted with power (and money is' the completest species of power) who do not stand pledged to use it exclusively for the general benefit. But the use of animal flesh and fermented liquors, directly militates with this equality of the rights of man. The peasant cannot gratify these fashionable cravings without leaving his family to starve. Without disease and war, those sweeping curtailers of population, pasturage would include a waste too great to he afforded. The labour requisite to support a family is far lighter[h] than is usually supposed. The peasantry work, not only for themselves, but for the aristocracy, the army, and the manufacturers. The advantage of a reform in diet is obviously greater than that of any other. It strikes at the root of the evil. To remedy the abuses of legislation, before we annihilate the propensities by which they are produced, is to suppose, that by taking away the effect, the cause will cease to operate. But the efficacy of this system depends entirely on the proselytism of individuals, and grounds its merits, as a benefit to the community, upon the total change of the dietetic habits in its members. It proceeds securely from a number of particular cases to one that is universal, and has this advantage over the contrary mode, that one error does not invalidate all that has gone before. Let not too much, however, be expected from this system. The healthiest among us is not exempt from hereditary disease. The most symmetrical, athletic,

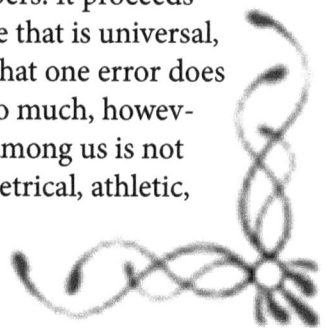

145

and long-lived, is a being inexpressibly inferior to what he would have been, had not the unnatural habits of his ancestors accumulated for him a certain portion of malady and deformity. In the most perfect specimen of civilized man, something is still found wanting by the physiological critic. Can a return to nature, then, instantaneously eradicate predispositions that have been slowly taking root in the silence of innumerable ages?—Indubitably not. All that I contend for is, that from the moment of the relinquishing all unnatural habits, no new disease is generated; and that the predisposition to hereditary maladies gradually perishes, for want of its accustomed supply. In cases of consumption, cancer, gout, asthma, and scrofula, such is the invariable tendency of a diet of vegetables and pure water. Those who may be induced by these remarks to give the vegetable system a fair trial, should in the first place, date the commencement of their practice, from the moment of their conviction. All depends upon breaking through a pernicious habit resolutely, and at once. Dr. Trotter[i] a asserts, that no drunkard was ever reformed by gradually relinquishing his dram. Animal flesh, in its effects on the human stomach, is analogous to a dram. lt is similar to the kind, though differing in the degree, of its operation. The proselyte to a pure diet must be warned to expect a temporary diminution of muscular strength. The subtraction of a powerful stimulus will suffice to account for this event. But it is only temporary, and is succeeded by an equable capability for exertion, far surpassing his. former various and fluctuating strength. Above all, he will acquire an easiness of breathing, by which stich exertion is performed, with a remarkable exemption from that painful and difficult panting now felt by almost every one, after hastily climbing an ordinary mountain. He will be equally capable of bodily exertion, or mental application, after as before his simple meal. He will feel none of the narcotic effects of ordinary diet. Irritability, the direct consequence of exhausting stimuli, would yield to the power of natural and tranquil impulses. He will no longer pine under the lethargy of ennui, that unconquerable weariness of life, more to be dreaded than death itself. He will escape the

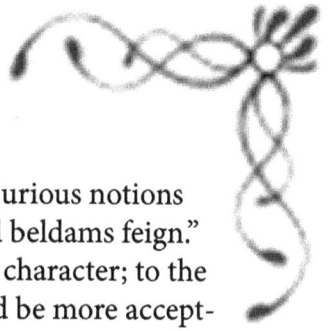

epidemic madness, which broods over its own injurious notions of the Deity, and "realizes the hell that priests and beldams feign." Every man forms as it were his god from his own character; to the divinity of one of simple habits, no offering would be more acceptable than the happiness of his creatures. He would be incapable of hating or persecuting others for the love of God. He will find, moreover, a system of simple diet to be a system of perfect epicurism. He will no longer be incessantly occupied in blunting and destroying those organs from which he expects his gratification. The pleasures of taste to be derived from a dinner of potatoes, beans, peas, turnips, lettuces, with a dessert of apples, gooseberries, strawberries, currants, raspberries, and, in winter, oranges, apples, and pears, is far greater than is supposed. Those who wait until they can eat this plain fare with the sauce of appetite will scarcely join with the hypocrital sensualist at a lord-mayor's feast, who declaims against the pleasures of the table. Solomon kept a thousand concubines, and owned in despair that all was vanity. The man whose happiness is constituted by the society of one amiable woman, would find some difficulty in sympapathizing with the disappointment of this venerable debauchee. I address myself not only to the young enthusiast, the ardent devotee of truth and virtue, the pure and passionate moralist, yet unvitiated by the contagion of the world. He will embrace a pure system, from its abstract truth, its beauty, its simplicity, and its promise of a wide-extended benefit; unless custom has turned poison into food, he will hate the brutal pleasures of the chase by instinct it will be a contemplation full of horror and disappointment to his mind, that beings capable of the gentlest and most admirable sympathies, should take delight in the death-pangs and last convulsions of dying animals. The elderly man, whose youth has been poisoned by intemperance, or who has lived with apparent moderation, and is afflicted with a variety of painful maladies, would find his account in a beneficial change, produced without the risk of poisonous medicines. The mother, to whom the perpetual restlessness of disease, and unaccountable deaths incident to her children, are the

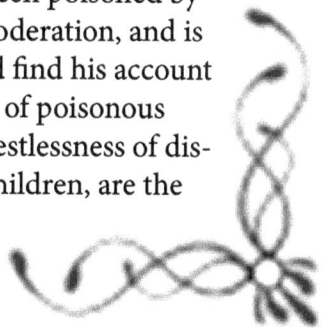

causes of incurable unhappiness, would on this diet experience the satisfaction of beholding their perpetual health and natural playfulness[j]. The most valuable lives are daily destroyed by diseases, that it is dangerous to palliate and impossible to cure by medicine. How much longer will man continue to pimp for the gluttony of death, his most insidious, implacable, and eternal foe?

----[a] Thus, from the sun's ethereal beam When bold Prometheus stole th' enlivening flame, Of fevers dire a ghastly brood, Till then unknown, th' unhappy fraud pursu'd; On earth their horrors baleful spread, And the pale monarch of the dead, Till then slow-moving to his prey, Precipitately rapid swept his way. Francis's Horace, Book i. Ode 3.

[b] Prometheus first killed an ox. Plin. Nat. Hist. lib. vii. sect. 57.

[c] Return to nature. Cadell, 1811.

[d] Cuvier, Leçons d' Anat. Comp. tom. iii. pages 169, 373, 443, 465, 480. Rees's Cyclopœdia, article Man.

[e] The necessity of resorting to some means of purifying water, and the disease which arises from its adulteration in civilized countries, is sufficiently apparent.—See Dr. Lambe's Reports on Cancer. I do not assert that the use of water is in itself unnatural, but that the unperverted palate would swallow no liquid capable of occasioning disease.

[f] Lambe's Reports on Cancer.

[g] Return to Nature, or Defence of Vegetable Regimen. Cadell, 1811.

[h] It has come under the author's experience, that some of the workmen on an embankment in North Wales, who, in consequence of the inability of the proprietor to pay them, seldom received their wages, have supported large families by cultivating small spots of sterile ground by moonlight In the notes to Pratt's Poem, "Bread, or the Poor," is an account of an industrious labourer, who, by working in a small garden, before and after his day's task, attained to an enviable state of independence.

[i] See Trotter on the Nervous Temperament.

^jSee Mr. N,,wton's book, His children are the most beautiful and healthy creatures it is possible to conceive; the girls are perfect models for a sculptor; their dispositions are also the most gentle and conciliating; the judicious treatment which they experience in other points, may be a correlative cause of this. In the first five years of their life, of 18,000 children that are born, 7,500 die of various diseases; and how many more of those that survive are rendered miserable by maladies not immediately mortal? The quality and quantity of a woman's milk are materially injured by the use of dead flesh. In an island, near Iceland, where no vegetables are to be got, the children invariably die of tetanus, before they are three weeks old, and the population is supplied from the main land.- Sir G. Mackemie's Hist. of Iceland. See also Emile, chap. i. p. 53, 54, 56.

Ἀλλὰ δράκοντας ἀξείς καλεῖτε καὶ παρδάλεις καὶ λέοντας, αὐτοὶ
δὲ μιαιφονεῖτε εἰς ὠμότητα καταλιπόντες ἐκείνοις οὐδέν. Ἐκείνοις μὲν
γὰρ ὁ φόνος τροφή, ὑμῖν δὲ ὄψον ἐστίν.

*   *   *   *   *   *   *   *   *

Ὅτι γὰρ οὐκ ἔστιν ἀνθρώπῳ κατὰ φύσιν τὸ σαρκοφαγεῖν, πρῶτον μὲν ἀπὸ
τῶν σωμάτων δηλοῦται τῆς κατασκευῆς. Οὐδενὶ γὰρ ἔοικε τὸ ἀνθρώπου
σῶμα τῶν ἐπὶ σαρκοφαγίᾳ γεγονότων, ἃ γρυπότης χείλεις, οὐκ ὀξύτης
ὄνυχος, ἃ τραχύτης ὀδόντων πρόσεστιν, ἃ κοιλίας εὐτονία, καὶ πνεύματος
θερμότης, τρέψαι καὶ κατεργάζεσθαι δυνατὴ τὸ βαρὺ καὶ κρεῶδες.
Ἀλλ' αὐτόθεν ἡ φύσις τῇ λειότητι τῶν ὀδόντων, καὶ τῇ σμικρότητι τοῦ
στόματος, καὶ τῇ μαλακότητι τῆς γλώσσης, καὶ τῇ πρὸς πέψιν
ἀμβλύτητι τοῦ πνεύματος, ἐξόμνυται τὴν σαρκοφαγίαν. Εἰ δὲ λέγεις
πεφυκέναι σεαυτὸν ἐπὶ τοιαύτην ἐδωδήν, ὃ βούλει φαγεῖν, πρῶτον αὐτὸς
ἀπόκτεινον· ἀλλ' αὐτός, διὰ σεαυτοῦ μὴ χρησάμενος κοπίδι, μηδὲ
τυχανῳ μηδὲ πελέκει, ἀλλὰ ὡς λύκοι, καὶ ἄρκτοι, καὶ λέοντες αὐτοὶ ὡς
ἐσθίουσι φονεύουσιν, ἄνελε δήγματι βοῦν, ἢ σώματι σῦν, ἢ ἄρνα ἢ λαγῶον
διάρρηξον, καὶ φάγε προσπεσὼν ἔτι ζῶντος ὡς ἐκεῖνα.

*   *   *   *   *   *   *   *   *

Ἡμεῖς δὲ οὕτως ἐν τῷ μιαιφόνῳ τρυφῶμεν, ὥστε ὄψον τὸ κρέας
προσαγορεύομεν, εἶτα ὄψων πρὸς αὐτὸ τὸ κρέας δεόμεθα, ἀναμιγνύντες
ἔλαιον, οἶνον, μέλι, γάρον, ὄξος, ἡδύσμασι Συριακοῖς, Ἀρραβικῖς
ὥσπερ ὄντως νεκρὸν ἐνταφιάζοντες. Καὶ γὰρ οὕτως αὐτῶν διαλυθέντων
καὶ μαλαχθέντων καὶ τρόπον τινὰ κρεοσαπέντων ἔργον ἐστὶ τὴν πέψιν
κρατῆσαι· καὶ διακρατηθείσης δὲ δεινὰς βαρύτητας καὶ νοσώδεις
ἀπεψίας.
Οὕτω τὸ πρῶτον ἄγριόν τι ζῶον ἐβρώθη καὶ κακέργον, εἶτα ὄρνις τις
ἢ ἰχθὺς εἵλκυστο· καὶ γευόμενον οὕτω καὶ προμελετῆσαν ἐν ἐκείνοις τὸ
νικῆν, ἐπὶ βοῦν ἐργάτην ἦλθε, καὶ τὸ κόσμιον πρόβατον, καὶ τὸν οἴκουρον
ἀλεκτρυόνα· καὶ κατὰ μικρὸν οὕτω τὴν ἀπληστίαν τονώσαντες, ἐπὶ
σφαγὰς ἀνθρώπων, καὶ φόνους καὶ πολέμους προῆλθον.

Πλουτ. περὶ τῆς σαρκοφαγίας.

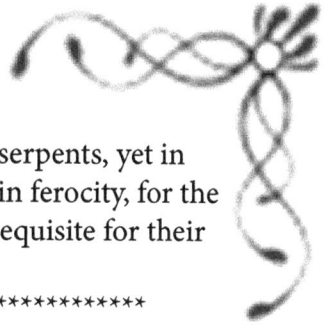

^A You apply the term wild to lions, panthers, and serpents, yet in you own savage slaughters, you far surpass them in ferocity, for the blood shed by them is a matter of necessity, and requisite for their subsistence.

****

That man is not by nature destined to devour animal food, is evident from the construction of the human frame, which bears no resemblance to wild beasts, or birds of prey. Man is not provided with claws or talons, with sharpness of fang, or tusk, so well adapted to tear and lacerate; nor is his stomach so well braced and muscular, nor Isis animal spirits so warm as to enable him to digest this solid mass of animal flesh. On the contrary, nature has made his teeth smooth, his mouth narrow, and his tongue soft; and has contrived, by the slowness of his digestion, to divert him from devouring a species of food so ill adapted to his frame and constitution. But if you still maintain, that such is your natural mode of subsistence, then follow nature in your mode of killing your prey, and employ neither knife, hammer, or hatchet, but like wolves, bears, and lions, seize an ox with your teeth, grasp a boar round the body, or tear asunder a lamb or a hare, and like the savage tribe, devour them still panting in the agonies of death.

****

We carry our luxury still farther, by the variety of sauces and seasonings which we add to our beastly banquets, mixing together oil, wine, honey, pickles, vinegar, and Syrian and Arabian ointments and perfumes, as if we intended to bury and embalm the carcases on which we feed. The difficulty of digesting such a mass of matter reduced in our stomachs to a state of liquefaction and putrefaction, is the source of endless disorders in the human frame. First of all, the wild mischievous animals were selected for food, and then the birds and fishes were dragged to slaughter; next the human appetite directed itself against the laborious ox, the useful and fleece-bearing sheep, and the cock, the guardian of the house. At last, by this preparatory discipline, man became matured for human massacres, slaughters, and wars.

THE END.

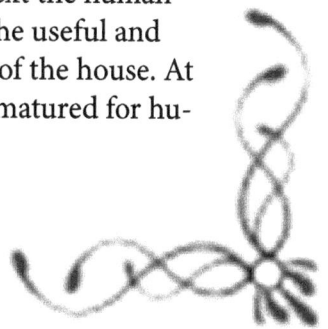

www.ingramcontent.com/pod-product-compliance
Lightning Source LLC
Chambersburg PA
CBHW070836100426
42813CB00003B/636